1

~Introducing Fiqh Series
Vol.3

Introducing the Fiqh of Fasting

(فقه الصوم)

Written and compiled by
SAFARUK Z. CHOWDHURY

AD-DUHA
LONDON 2009

First edition 2007
Second edition 2008

Updated Edition 2009

An educational publication from Ad-Duha London
Third Floor, 42 Fieldgate Street
London E1 1ES
E: info@duha.org.uk
W: www.duha.org.uk
T: 07891 421 925

Contents Page

4

TABLE OF ABBREVIATIONS

Art.   = article

Bk.   = book

pp.   = pages

ˋ   = the Arabic letter ع

ʿ   = the Arabic letter ء

اه .   = 'end of quote' where a cited textual segment in Arabic ends.

s: = additional comments made by the translator

TABLE OF SYMBOLS

= *hadith* number

(…)   = contains transliteration of Arabic terms

[…]   = contains additions by the translator

… / […]   = ellipsis where a textual segment is elided and omitted in translation by the translator

{…}   = enclosure of a Qur'anic verse in translation

§   = section

Bab: al-Sawm fi Ramadan:
Introducing the Fiqh of Fasting

الحمد لله رب العالمين، والصلاة والسلام على خاتم الأنبياء والمرسلين،
المبعوث رحمة للعالمين نبينا و حبيبنا محمد وعلى آله وصحبه أجمعين

The following is only the basic rulings for an individual regarding the act of fasting and omits many aspects otherwise found in the books of *fiqh*. It is merely a quick and easy reference especially for Ramadan fasts and not a full guide or manual. Much of it is based on Imam al-Shurunbulali's excellent primer on devotional rulings entitled *Nur al-Idah* with supplementary notes from his own marginal commentary entitled *Maraqi al-Falah* as well as other Hanafi legal commentaries. Included too are answers to a number of actual questions put forward by the public which highlight common scenarios that present themselves during the fast in order to provide general answers for reference purposes. It is hoped this will be of some benefit to those who use it and we ask Allah to accept this humble effort for service of His Religion. *Amin.*

§1. Why Muslims Fast

There are number of reasons as to why Muslims fast answered from the noble verse in the Holy Qur'an itself. Allah the exalted says in *surat* al-Baqara:183-188:

{*O ye who believe! Fasting is prescribed to you as it was prescribed to those before you, that ye may (learn) self-restraint; (Fasting) for a fixed number of days; but if any of you is ill, or on a journey, the prescribed number (Should be made up) from days later. For those who can do it (With hardship), is a ransom, the feeding of one that is indigent. But he that will give more, of his own free will,- it is better for him. And it is better for you that ye fast, if ye only knew. Ramadhan is the (month) in which was sent down the Qur'an, as a guide to mankind, also clear (Signs) for guidance and judgment (Between right and wrong). So every one of you who is present (at his home) during that month should spend it in fasting, but if anyone is ill, or on a journey, the prescribed period (Should be made up) by days later. Allah intends every facility for you; He does not want to put to difficulties. (He wants you) to complete the prescribed period, and to glorify Him in that He has guided you; and perchance ye shall be grateful. When My servants ask thee concerning Me, I am indeed close (to them): I listen to the prayer of every suppliant when he calleth on Me: Let them also, with a will, Listen to My call, and believe in Me: That they may walk in the right way. Permitted to you, on the night of the fasts, is the approach to your wives. They are your garments and ye are their garments. Allah knoweth what ye used to do secretly among yourselves; but He turned to you and forgave you; so now associate with them, and seek what Allah Hath ordained for you, and eat and drink, until the white thread of dawn appear to you distinct from its black thread; then complete your fast Till the night appears; but do not associate with your wives while ye are in retreat in the mosques. Those are Limits (set by) Allah: Approach not nigh thereto. Thus doth Allah make clear His Signs to men: that they may learn self-restraint. And do not eat up your property among yourselves for vanities, nor use it as bait for the judges, with intent that ye may eat up wrongfully and knowingly a little of (other) people's property*}.[1]

From the verse above, the answer to why the question why Muslims fast is three fold:

[1] It is a command from Allah to those who profess faith. Being addressed by the description *ya ayyuha'lladhina amanu* ('O believers') indicates that Allah reminds those who claim to believe in Him, His Messenger and the Message of Islam (*risala*) that a religious duty has been laid down. > thus, the first and foremost reason why Muslims fast is that it is based on Allah's expressive command. His expressive command grounds the duty to fast, i.e. it is the basis and reason.[2]

[2] Fasting is not new to Islam but part of religious prescriptions in earlier nations (*al-umum al-sabiqa*) as part of the practice chosen by Allah for the previous Prophets (*al-anbiya'*) such as Ibrahim, Moses, Jesus, etc. Thus, fasting is within the tradition established and chosen by Allah for the righteous and God-fearing.[3]

[3] Another reason why fasting is performed is that it is a means of securing/acquiring *taqwa* (from the word *wiqaya* [وقاية = 'protection', 'prevention']) which variously translates as 'fear', 'piety', 'God-consciousness'.[4] Human beings naturally forget,

---

[1] A. Y. Ali translation.

[2] al-Tabarani, *Tafsir*, 1:132.

[3] Ibid., 1:132.

[4] Note as well the *hadith* that "fasting is a shield" (الصوم جنة) as mentioned by Imam al-Tirmidhi as part of a longer *hadith* in his *Sunan* (#2616) and many others. Thus fasting prevents one from iniquity and shields him from external intrusion.

stray, fall into error, succumb to the overwhelming pressures of their *nafs* (ego-soul) or become heedless of what their ultimate priorities are because of ignorance, sin or lure and temptations of the *dunya*. Ramadan is a month to prevent this and to put a stop to it – a 30 day training of the individual to battle h/her weaknesses and steer towards awareness of Allah in all spheres. Hence, it is no surprise that Ramadan has a robust regimen which includes:

a. Getting up to eat the pre-dawn meal (*al-suhur*).
b. Restraining one's self during the day from a host of things.
c. Reciting the Qur'an.
d. Standing in the *tarawih* prayer.
e. Performing the night vigil prayer (*tahajjud*).
f. Other, etc...

Thus, the whole month is about connecting to Allah, waking up from heedlessness and spiritual lethargy as well as altering our fixed patterns of worldly life. We fast because Allah has commanded us to and as believers we submit to it entirely. Fasting is a means chosen by Allah to secure and acquire *taqwa*. We ask Allah to accept our fast and to allow us to acquire *taqwa* therein. *Amin.*

[§2a] The basic definition of fasting

***

FASTING (*al-siyam*): "It is defined as refraining from allowing anything to enter the stomach (*al-batn*) – or anything that takes the ruling of the stomach – whether intentionally or unintentionally. It is also defined as abstaining from sexual gratification along with the intention of fasting for the person who fits the criteria for fasting."[5]

هو الإمساك نهارا عن إدخال شيء عمدا أو خطأ بطنا أو ماله حكم الباطن وعن شهوة الفرج بنية من أهله

[§2b] Intention to Fast

أما القسم الذي لا يشترط فيه تعيين النية و لا تبييتها فهو أداء رمضان...

"As for the type of fasting for which it is not conditional to be specific in the intention, nor to make the intention at night before the dawn, then it includes fasting the month of Ramadan".[6]

- Thus:

1. Ramadan fasts do not require an intention to specify what type of fast it is and may be made from between the night before up until the *dahwat al-kubra* (ضحوة الكبرى)* the next day based on the *hadith* of the Messenger of Allah (saw) from Salama b. al-Akwa` (ra) where the Prophet commanded the people to fast on the `Ashura' day:

---

[5] al-Shurunbulali, *Nur al-Idah*, 1:55.
[6] Ibid, 1:56.

أمر النبي صلى الله عليه وسلم رجلاً من أسلم : (أن أذن في الناس : أن من كان أكل
فليصم بقية يومه، ومن لم يكن أكل فليصم، فإن اليوم يوم عاشوراء) .

"The Prophet (saw) commanded a man who had embraced Islam to announce to the people that whoever has eaten, to fast the rest of the day and that whoever has not yet eaten to fast because it is the day of `Ashura'."[7]

*[**Note**: The way to calculate the *dahwat al-kubra* is to total the time between Fajr and Maghrib and then divide by half].

2. Ramadan *qada'* (make-up) fast does require an intention.

[§2c] Types of Invalid Fasts

It is important to remember at least 4 scenarios when it comes to fasts:

1. A fast that is invalidated and requires a *kaffara* (penalty/expiation) and *qada'* (make up fast).

2. A fast that is invalidated and requires a *qada'* only.

3. A fast that is broken and requires a *qada'* only.

4. A fast that is **missed** (not done at all) and requires a *qada'* only.

---

[7] Bukhari, *Sahih* (#2007) and Muslim, *Sahih* (#1135). Because the people would only have made intention on the actual day of the fast they had been ordered and not the night before. Hence it must be permitted to make an intention to fast on the day of the fast.

[§3] General rules related to that
which does not invalidate the Fast

***

General Rule 1: "If anyone eats, drinks or has sexual intercourse forgetting that he is fasting, this does not invalidate the fast".[8]

ما لو أكل أو شرب أو جامع ناسيا...

إذا نسي فأكل وشرب فليتم صومه، فإنما أطعمه الله وسقاه

"If a person eats or drinks forgetfully, he should continue to complete his fast. There is no *qada'* on him for indeed Allah will fccd and nourish him..."[9]

- Thus, anything done <u>forgetfully</u> does not invalidate the fast such as:

1. Eating forgetfully.
2. Drinking forgetfully.
3. Having sex forgetfully.

- A person however should stop doing what they are doing immediately when they realise that and continue fasting as normal.

General Rule 2: anything done <u>unintentionally</u> or involuntarily does not invalidate the fast such as:[10]

1. Vomiting.
2. Coughing (e.g. blood).

---

[8] al-Shurunbulali, *Nur al-Idah*, 1:58.
[9] Bukhari, *Sahih* (#1933) and Muslim, *Sahih* (#1155).
[10] al-Shurunbulali, *Nur al-Idah*, 1:58.

3. Yawning.
4. Sweating.
5. Breaking wind.
6. Sneezing.
7. Inhaling smoke unintentionally (e.g. of a cigarette, shisha, fire, incense).
8. Bed-wetting.

General Rule 3: anything exiting the body does not invalidate the fast such as:

1. Tears (e.g. when crying).
2. Blood (e.g. from a wound, etc.).
3. Pus (e.g. from an old wound).
4. Sweat (e.g. from extreme heat and exercise).
5. Mucus (e.g. from flu, illness, etc.).
6. Wind (e.g. from flatulence).
7. Excrement (e.g. diahorrea).
8. Urine (e.g. from incontinence).
9. Milk (e.g. from breastfeeding).
10. Vomit (e.g. from sickness).
11. Discharge (e.g. from a wound, surgery, etc).

- Thus, medical realities like blood tests, blood donation, sampling, etc. do not invalidate the fast.

General Rule 4: anything applied on the body parts or skin does not break the fast such as:[11]

1. Gels (hair and shower gels).
2. Oils.
3. Creams.
4. Fragrances (hairsprays, cologne, body-sprays, etc.).
5. Soaps.
6. Shampoos.

---

[11] Ibid, 1:59.

7. Cosmetics (lipsticks, eyeliners, mascara, foundation etc.).
8. Tanning products.

- Thus, medical realities like ultra sound scans are permitted and do not break the fast; therapeutic procedures like massages are also permitted and do not break the fast as well as tanning procedures in salon.

General Rule 5: "With regards to any cavity of the stomach, or any opening of the head, if either is administered with dry medicine, then the fast is not invalidated. According to Abu Hanifa, if both areas are treated with wet medicine, then the fast is invalidated although Abu Yusuf and al-Shaybani differed. Most of the scholars are of the opinion that what is of concern is whether the medicine actually reaches the stomach or brain."[12]

وفي الجائفة والآمة إذا داواهما بدواء يابس لا يفسد صومه وإذا داواهما بدواء رطب يفسد صومه عند أبي حنيفة خلافا لهما وأكثر المشايخ اعتبر الوصول إلى الجوف...

- Thus, if something enters the body through the skin and does not reach the stomach, intestines or brain, the fast is not invalidated such as:

1. Injections (insulin, pain injections, etc. as long they are not directly inserted into the stomach).

2. Patches (nicotine patches, hormone patches, therapy patches, etc.).

3. Drips, diffusion bags, saline bags, etc.

---

[12] al-Bukhari, *al-Muhit al-Burhani*, 3:348

[§4] General rules related to that which invalidates the Fast and requires both a *kaffara* and a *qada'* Fast

***

جاء رجل إلى النبي صلى الله عليه وسلم فقال: هلكت، قال : (وما شأنك) . قال: وقعت على امرأتي في رمضان، فقال: (هل تجد ما تعتق رقبة) . قال: لا، قال: (فهل تستطيع أن تصوم شهرين متتابعين) . قال: لا، قال: (فهل تستطيع أن تطعم ستين مسكينا) . قال : لا أجد، فأتي النبي صلى الله عليه وسلم بعرق فيه تمر، فقال : (خذ هذا فتصدق به) . فقال: أعلى أفقر منا؟ ما بين لابتيها أفقر منا، ثم قال: (خذه فأطعمه أهلك)

"A man came to the Prophet (saw) and cried: 'I'm destroyed!' – or words to that effect – 'I had intercourse with my wife in Ramadan. The Prophet asked: **'are you able to free a slave?'** he replied: 'no'. The Prophet asked: **'are you able to fast two months consecutively?'** he replied: 'no'. The Prophet then asked: **'Are you able to feed sixty poor persons?'** The man replied: 'I can't'. So the Prophet (saw) came to him with a basket of dates and said: **'take this and make charity with it'**. The man said: 'none is poorer between these two mountains than us.' The Prophet said: **'Take it and feed your family'**."[13]

General rule 6: "If a person who is fasting does something willingly and intentionally without being compelled or forced, then the fast is categorically invalidated and it will require a *kaffara* and *qada'* fast."[14]

اذا فعل الصائم شيئا منها طائعا متعمدا غير مضطر لزمه القضاء والكفارة...

- Thus, if someone deliberately eats, drinks and has sexual intercourse, or does any type of action that willingly allows any food, water, or nutrient to enter the body will automatically invalidate the fast.

---

[13] Bukhari, *Sahih* (#6711) and Muslim, *Sahih* (#1111).
[14] al-Shurunbulali, *Nur al-Idah*, 1:59.

General rule 7: "If a person eats or drinks anything that provides nourishment or is used as a medicine then he is liable for *qada'* as well as *kaffara*."[15]

لو أكل أو شرب ما يتغذى به أو ما يداوي به فعليه القضاء و الكفارة...

- Thus, taking pills, supplements, common prescription drugs as well as nourishing products will not be permitted.

---

[15] al-Marghinani, *al-Hidaya*, 1:134.

[§5] General rules related to that which invalidates the Fast and requires only a *qada'* Fast

***

General rule 8: "Whatever reaches the stomach or the brain from any of the openings of the body such as through the nose, the ears and the rear because of an enema or drops into the nose and car, <u>then if it reaches the stomach or the brain, the fast will be invalidated.</u>"[16]

وما وصل إلى الجوف أو إلى الدماغ من المخارق الأصلية كالأنف والأذن والدبر بأن استعط
أو احتقن أو أقطر في أذنه فوصل إلى الجوف أو إلى الدماغ فسد صومه

- Thus, if anything is entered or administered through the ears, throat and nose and <u>it can or does reach the brain or stomach</u>, then the fast is invalidated such as:

  1. Nasal medicine (e.g. sprays and drops).
  2. Ear medicines (e.g. drops).
  3. Throat medicines (pills, liquids, etc.).

General Rule 9: If anything enters the vagina or anus invalidates the fast requiring a *qada'* fast only such as:[17]

  1. Water.
  2. Solids or liquid medicines.
  3. Objects.

- Medical realities include vaginal examinations and rectal examinations.

General Rule 10: "Or if smoke is inhaled into the throat intentionally."[18]

---

[16] al-Kasani, *al-Bada'i` al-Sana'i`*, 2:93.
[17] al-Shurunbulali, *Nur al-Idah*, 1:60.

أو أدخل حلقة دخانا بصنعه...

- Thus, <u>intentionally</u> inhaling smoke such that it enters the mouth or nose and down the throat invalidates the fast such as:

  1. Tobacco smoke.
  2. Shisha smoke.
  3. Incense smoke (e.g. agarbatti, etc.).

General Rule 11: If anything <u>accidentally</u> passes down the throat that could in principle be avoided invalidates the fast requiring a *qada'* fast only such as:[19]

  1. Gargling water during *wudu'* that accidentally passes down the throat.
  2. Accidentally swallowing rain water.
  3. Accidentally swallowing snow water.
  4. Accidentally swallowing shower water.

General Rule 12: If one acts on a mistake or accident thinking something was the case but in reality it was not, then this invalidates the fast and will require a *qada'* fast only such as:

  1. Mistakenly breaking fast earlier than the time thinking it was the actual time.

  2. Mistakenly eating at *suhur* time when in actual fact the time of Fajr had started.

---

[18] Ibid, 1:61.
[19] Ibid, 1:60.

General Rule 13: Anything that does not involve a complete act of sex or full reciprocal sexual gratification invalidates the fast and requires only a *qada'* fast such as:[20]

1. Masturbation.
2. Emission of semen without sexual intercourse.
3. Explicit sexual behaviour without penetration.

General Rule 14: Eating something not normally eaten, or what does not nourish the body or benefit it in any way invalidates the fast requiring a *qada'* fast such as:

1. Eating salts.
2. Eating stones.
3. Eating raw ingredients.
4. Eating paper, cotton, etc.
5. Eating metals.
6. Eating soils.

---

[20] Ibid, 1:60-61.

[§6] General rules related to that which is disliked (*makruh*) when fasting but do not invalidate the Fast

***

General rule 15: "Tasting something without any valid reason [is disliked]".[21]

ذوق الشئ بلا عذر...

- Thus tasting food when cooking, using toothpaste, mouthwashes, mouth sprays, etc. would be disliked to use due to the taste in them.

General Rule 16: "[...] exposing the fast to an act that will invalidate it".[22]

...تعريض الصوم للفساد

- Thus, actions such as the following and many others are disliked as they may dispose a person to break their fast:

  1. Chewing something,
  2. Tasting something,
  3. Gathering the saliva in the mouth in order to swallow it,
  4. Kissing and caressing one's spouse if one is not sure if h/she can stop going all the way.
  5. This also includes avoiding anything or any action by which a person can accuse another of eating or not be in a state a fasting (e.g. eating and drinking openly).

---

[21] Ibid, 1:63.
[22] al-Marghinani, *al-Hidaya*, 1:135.

General Rule 17: "Any action believed to weaken a person during the fast".[23]

و ما ظن أنه يضعفه...

- Thus, while fasting, <u>if able to</u>, one should avoid such things as:

1. Exercising rigorously as it can be rearranged for another time in the day.
2. Extended periods of sports (e.g. long training sessions).
3. Undergoing additional and long medical tests (e.g. giving blood).
4. Doing anything strenuous that can be avoided.

---

[23] al-Shurunbulali, *Nur al-Idah*, 1:60.

[§7] The recommended (*mustahabb*) aspects of Fasting

***

- There are three recommended things to do during the fast. <u>Failing this will not invalidate the fast</u> but the reward and blessing will be lost. They are:

[1] Waking up before the pre-dawn meal (*suhur*):

قوله تسحروا قد ذكرنا أنه أمر ندب بالإجماع قوله في السحور قال شيخنا رحمه الله روينا بفتح السين وضمها وهو بالضم الفعل وبالفتح اسم ما يتسحر به كالوضوء والسعوط والحنوط ونحوها قوله بركة قد ذكروا فيها معان الأول إنه يبارك فيه باليسير منه بحيث يحصل به الإعانة على الصوم ويدل عليه قوله ولو بجرعة ماء ولو بتمرة ونحو ذلك ويكون ذلك بالخاصية كما بورك في الثريد والطعام إذا هدى في الحرارة واجتماع الجماعة على الطعام لقوله اجتمعوا على طعامكم يبارك لكم فيه الثاني يراد بالبركة نفي التبعة فيه وقد ذكر صاحب الفردوس من حديث أبي هريرة ثلاثة لا يحاسب عليها العبد اكلة السحور وما أفطر عليه وما أكل مع الإخوان الثالث يراد بالبركة القوة عن الصيام وغيره من أعمال النهار الرابع يراد بالبركة الرخصة والصدقة وهو الزيادة في الأكل على الأكل عند الإفطار كما كان أولا ثم نسخ واصل البركة في اللغة الزيادة والنماء وقال عياض قد تكون هذه البركة ما يتفق للمتسحر من ذكر أو صلاة أو استغفار وغيره من زيادات الأعمال التي لولا القيام للسحور لكان الإنسان نائما عنها وتاركا لها وتجديد النية للصوم ليخرج من الاختلاف وقال ابن دقيق العيد هذه البركة يجوز أن تعودوا إلى الأمور الأخروية فإن اتامة السنة توجب الأجر وزيادته ويحتمل أن تعود إلى الأمور الدنيوية كقوة البدن على الصوم وتيسيره من غير أضرار بالصائم قال ومما يعلل به استحباب السحور المخالفة لأهل الكتاب لأنه ممتنع عندهم وهذا أحد الوجوه المقتضية بالزيادة في الأجور الأخروية...

"[The Prophet's] statement 'eat the pre-dawn meal' which we mentioned is a recommended command according to consensus [...] it being a blessing (*baraka*) has many meanings as mentioned [by the scholars]. **The First**: it is a blessing in that it makes [fasting] easy by aiding the fasting [...] **The Second**: it being a blessing means it negates any difficulty [...] **The third**: it being a blessing means it gives strength to fast or do actions during the day or other such things [...] **The Fourth**: it being a blessing means it is a ease and a form of charity which is an increase to eating during the *iftar* [...] [Imam Qadi] `Iyad said that through this blessing perhaps a person who wakes up for the pre-dawn meal will engage in remembrance of Allah (*dhikr*), or perform extra prayers or seek forgiveness or other such additional actions which if he did not wake up for the pre-dawn meal, would otherwise have missed through sleeping or leaving it..."[24]

[2] **To delay the pre-dawn meal**: because the Messenger of Allah (saw) said: "From `A'isha (ra) who said that: three things are from the Prophethood. Hastening the *iftar*, delaying the *suhur* and placing the right hand over the left hand in the prayer..."[25]

عن عائشة قالت ثلاث من النبوة تعجيل الإفطار وتأخير السحور ووضع الرجل يده اليمنى
على اليسرى في الصلاة

[3] **Hastening in breaking the fast**: based upon the *hadith* mentioned above.

---

[24] al-`Ayni, *Umdat al-Qari Sharh Sahih al-Bukhari*, 10:301 (#3291).
[25] al-Bayhaqi, *al-Sunan al-Kubra*, 2:29; al-Mundhiri, *al-Targhib wa' l-Tarhib*, 1:151 and al-Haythami, *Majma` al-Zawa'id*, 2:108.

[8] The *Kaffara* and its basic Rulings

***

والكفارة تحرير رقبة ولو كانت غير مؤمنة فإن عجز عنه صام شهرين متتابعين ليس فيهما يوم عيد ولا أيام التشريق فإن لم يستطع الصوم أطعم ستين مسكينا يغديهم ويعشيهم غداء وعشاء مشبعين أو غداءين أو عشاءين أو عشاء وسحورا أو يعطي كل فقير نصف صاع من بر أو دقيقه أو سويقه أو صاع تمر أو شعير أو قيمته تداخل الكفارات. وكفت كفارة واحدة عن جماع وأكل متعدد في أيام لم يتخلله تكفير ولو من رمضانين على الصحيح فإن تخلل التكفير لا تكفي كفارة واحدة في ظاهر الرواية.

"The expiation involves the freeing of a slave even if it is a non-Muslim. And if one is unable to do that, he must fast two consecutive months that do not coincide with either the two 'Ids or the days of Tashriq. Failing this, then the expiation is to feed 60 unfortunate people who are to be treated to lunch and dinner [at their respective times] so that they are content or [the unfortunate persons] are fed two lunches and two dinners or fed a dinner and a pre-dawn meal. It is also permitted to offer each unfortunate person half a *sa`* of wheat, flour or one *sa`* of dates or barely or the value equal to [the above items]. One expiation suffices for sexual intercourse committed on different days as well as eating on different days throughout Ramadan even though these are days of Ramadan of two different years. If however, an expiation has occurred between two acts, then one offer of expiation is not sufficient and this is the most evident view on the matter."[26]

- The matter of *kaffara* is thus very serious with required particulars.[27]

- The sequence is as follows:

[26] al-Shurunbulali, *Nur al-Idah*, 1:54.
[27] Refer to Alahazrat Imam Ahmed Reza Khan's *al-Fatawa al-Ridawiyya*, 10:595-596 for details.

1. To free any slave (*raqaba*) - Muslim or non-Muslim.

2. Failing this (perhaps due to lack of access), two consecutive months (*shahrayn mutatabi`ayn*) of fasting that must not encompass the two `Ids or the 11th, 12th and 13th Dhu 'l-Hijja (= *ayyam al-tashriq*).[28]

3. Failing this (perhaps due to illness or old age) to do either of the following:

A.	B.	C.	D.
60 poor/unfortunate individuals (*miskin*) must be properly fed both at lunch and dinner.	60 poor/unfortunate individuals treated to two lunches each.	60 poor/unfortunate individuals treated to two dinners each.	60 poor/unfortunate individuals treated to dinner and a pre-dawn meal (*sahur*).

4. Failing this, to give 60 persons equivalent to 1 *sa`* (= 1.6kg) of wheat or flour, or 1 *sa`* (= 3.2kg) of dates or barely.

- The *kaffara* is to fast 60 consecutive days without excuse. > if one is able, one must do it.

- In the Hanafi School, there is no latitude given for the choice of *kaffara* to make – it must be followed in sequence.

---

[28] al-Shurunbulali, *Maraqi al-Falah*, p.244.

[§9] General rules related to Exemption from Fasting

The following are exempted from fasting during Ramadan but will have to make up for it afterwards (i.e. perform a *qada'* fast):

1. Anyone who fears the fast will worsen the illness.[29]

2. Anyone who has a legitimate fear (of loss of limbs, life, mind, health).[30]

3. Anyone who suffers severe and extreme thirst.[31]

4. Anyone who suffers severe and unbearable bodily pains (e.g. severe arthritis, migraines).[32]

5. Anyone who is travelling on a journey.[33]

6. Anyone who is elderly and extremely feeble.

7. When a mother fears for her child's health and her own.[34]

8. Anyone on their menstrual cycle (period).[35]

9. Anyone who is a wet-nurse.

---

[29] al-Shurunbulali, *Maraqi al-Sa`adat*, p.134.
[30] Ibid, p.134.
[31] Ibid, p.134.
[32] Ibid, p.134.
[33] Ibid, p.135.
[34] Ibid, p.134.
[35] Ibid, p.134.

[10] The *Fidya* (Monetary Compensation)

***

Below is a Q & A on *Fidya* written by this author some years go outlining the basic rulings:

Q. My father has severe diabetes which means he has to take insulin and he is very weak. What does he have to do during Ramadan and can he fast?

A.

If your father attempts to fast by say changing his insulin regime to a different time in order to accommodate the fast but yet he is unable to do so and has to take his insulin, then he may not fast and make it up later as *qada'* (make up fast) when he recovers or feels better. This is the case if his illness is not permanent and absolutely chronic or terminal.

If however his health is too frail and weak to such an extent that he is actually not able to fast then he is given the dispensation (*rukhsa*) to pay what is called the *fidya* ('expiatory payment'). This is from the mercy of Allah. The value of the *fidya* is 1.6kg of wheat or its equivalent (which is the same as that of *Sadqat al-Fitr*)[36] and is around £2.50-£3.00 in the U.K at the moment. Imam al-Bukhari al-Hanafi writes in *al-Muhit al-Burhani*:

"Our teachers say that if the one who is ill knows that he will eventually die[37] and that was prolonged such that he was able to appoint an official testament executor on his behalf then in this condition

قال مشايخنا إذا كان مريض يعلم أن آخره الموت وامتد ذلك حتى أمكنه الإيصاء يجعل في هذه الحالة بمنزلة الشيخ الفاني...

---

[36] al-Marghinani, *al-Hidaya*, 1:210.
[37] i.e. terminally ill such that recovery is not likely.

he is considered the same as the extremely old [who can pay the *fidya*]..."[38]

However, it should be remembered that if your father becomes capable of fasting again (i.e. he feels he is able to fast easily in say when Ramadan falls on extremely shorter days or later in the year), he will have to make up for the missed fasts *despite* paying the *fidya* as mentioned in *al-Fatawa al-Hindiyya*:

"Regarding those who are aged (advanced in years): the extremely old who are unable to fast will feed the food to the poor for each day of the fast [they miss] as they would do in the case of the *kaffara* (atonement). This was mentioned in *al-Hidaya*. The same holds for those who are infirm – as mentioned in *al-Siraj al-Wahhaj* – who are deteriorating by the day until death. This is mentioned in *al-Bahr al-Ra'iq*. Thus, the person may choose to pay the *fidya* once in the first part of Ramadan or in the last part as mentioned in *al-Nahr al-Fa'iq*. However, if he is able to fast again after being able to pay the *fidya* then the ruling of the *fidya* is overruled and it becomes obligatory on him to fast. This is mentioned in *al-*

وَمِنْهَا كِبَرُ السِّنَّ فَالشَّيْخُ الْفَانِي الذي لَا يَقْدِرُ على الصِّيَام يُفْطِرُ وَيُطْعِمُ لِكُلِّ يَوْمٍ مِسْكِينًا كما يُطْعِمُ في الْكَفَّارَةِ كَذَا في الْهِدَايَةِ وَالْعَجُوزُ مِثْلُهُ كَذَا في السِّرَاجِ الْوَهَّاجِ وهو الذي كُلُّ يَوْمٍ في نَقْصٍ إلَى أَنْ يَمُوتَ كَذَا في الْبَحْرِ الرَّائِقِ ثُمَّ إنْ شَاءَ أَعْطَى الْفِدْيَةَ في أَوَّلِ رَمَضَانَ بِمَرَّةٍ وَإِنْ شَاءَ أَخَّرَهَا إلَى آخِرِهِ كَذَا في النَّهْرِ الْفَائِقِ وَلَوْ قَدَرَ على الصِّيَام بَعْدَ ما فَدَى بَطَلَ حُكْمُ الْفِدَاءِ الذي فَدَاهُ حتى يَجِبَ عليه الصَّوْمُ هَكَذَا في النِّهَايَةِ...

---

[38] al-Bukhari, *al-Muhit al-Burhani*, 2:361.

Nihaya..."[39]

And Allah knows best.

---

[39] al-Nizam et al, *al-Fatawa al-Hindiyya*, 2:207.

[11] Miscellaneous rulings for pregnant women and Wet-Nurses

***

وَالِاجْتِهَادُ غَيْرُ مُجَرَّدِ الْوَهْمِ بَلْ هُو غَلَبَةُ ظَنٍّ عن أَمَارَةٍ أو تَجْرِبَةٍ أو بِإِخْبَارِ طَبِيبٍ مُسْلِمٍ غَيْرِ
ظَاهِرِ الْفِسْقِ كَذَا في فَتْحِ الْقَدِيرِ ... وَمِنْهَا حَبَلُ الْمَرْأَةِ وَإِرْضَاعُهَا الْحَامِلُ وَالْمُرْضِعُ إذَا
خَافَتَا على أَنْفُسِهِمَا أو وَلَدِهِمَا أَفْطَرَتَا وَقَضَتَا وَلَا كَفَّارَةَ عَلَيْهِمَا كَذَا في الْخُلَاصَةِ

"And a person's utmost effort (*ijtihad*) is not mere supposition or whim rather it is the least amount of doubt from clear unmistakable signs, past experiences and the notice from a genuine Muslim doctor who is not openly sinning as mentioned in *Fath al-Qadir* [...] another example of one who is excused from fasting are the pregnant women and the wet-nurses who both have a genuine fear for themselves and the child may break the fast and make up for it later; there will be no *kaffara* for them as mentioned in *al-khulasa*...["40]

- Thus:

1. Unless due to a genuine fear, pregnant women must fast (§9).

2. If due to a real fear, illness and complication for the baby, she is unable to fast then she must make it up later in the year (§9).

3. Breastfeeding does not invalidate the fast (Rule 3).

4. *Tarawih* prayer may not be skipped unless with a genuine reason (chronic fatigue, bad health, illness, etc.) as it is a *sunna mu'akkada* ('emphatic sunna').

[40] See *al-Fatawa al-Hindiyya*, 1:207.

5. Even if not fasting, a woman (like a man) ought not to eat or drink in front of others (Rule 16).

6. It is permitted for a pregnant woman to attach pain patches on her arm or take pain/insulin injections during the fast (Rule 5).

[12] Miscellaneous rulings:

***

1. Backbiting does not invalidate the fast.

2. Watching unlawful things does not invalidate the fast.

3. Swearing does not invalidate the fast.

4. Arousing oneself does not invalidate the fast.

5. Thinking of unlawful things does not invalidate the fast.

6. Visiting an unlawful place does not invalidate the fast.

However, all the above actions are **not** permitted and are sinful.

7. Wet dreams do not invalidate the fast.

8. Watching TV does not invalidate the fast.

9. Swallowing blood from a gum bleed does not invalidate the fast.

10. Shaving, trimming and grooming hairs while fasting does not invalidate it.

11. Merely swallowing the taste of food without anything actually being there does not invalidate the fast.

12. Kissing one's spouse does not invalidate the fast.

13. Inserting one's finger into the ear during *wudu'* does not invalidate the fast.

[13] Common Scenarios

Below are common scenarios during the fast and have been outlined through written Q & A by the author. There are two parts: [1] general or common scenarios related to the fast and [2] common medical scenarios.

***

1. Fasting and Perfumes

Q. I recently went shopping in da west end and walked into Selfridges while i was also fasting. Does this affect my fasting? And do i have to re-do it?

A.

It is well known that wearing nice clothes, looking smart and clean as well as perfuming ourselves are all highly recommended and hence rewardable acts. The generality of these recommendations are not specified (restricted) by the fast in Ramadan. Islam is a beautiful and bounteous religion and Allah (swt) likes to see His bounty reflected in His servant's show of gratitude.[41] Fasting does not mean we cannot dress well or smell nice with permitted types of fragrances. Moreover, the blessed month of Ramadan does not mean one cannot enjoy spending time in shopping (say for `Id) or other perhaps necessary endeavours.

With regard to the question, intentionally inhaling fragrances (e.g. to see if they are to one's liking before buying them) or spraying fragrances (say, after exiting the

---

[41] The Prophet (saw) said:

"Allah loves to see the effects of his blessings on his servants..." al-Tirmidhi, *Sunan* (#2819).

إن الله يحب أن يرى أثر نعمته على عبده...

mens or ladies toilets) while fasting do not invalidate the fast.[42] The great Judge of Egypt Imam al-Shurunbulali writes:

"Or if smoke enters his throat intentionally. This is because one is unable to prevent it from entering; hence it becomes like wetness or dampness (moisture) that remains in the mouth after rinsing water through the nose when it enters the mouth filling it up. What we have mentioned indicates that whoever deliberately inhales any form of smoke and it enters into the throat in whichever way, the smoke entering invalidates the fast regardless of whether the smoke is fragrant smoke or perfumed smoke or anything else like it. So whoever serenades himself with incense smoke has done bad to himself. If one inhaled fragrance by intentionally drawing it towards one's self and smelling it's smoke, whilst remembering that one is fasting, then one's fast would become invalid due to being able to prevent it from entering any body cavity or the brain. This is something regarding which many people are

(أو دخل حلقه دخان بلا صنعه) لعدم قدرته على الامتناع عنه فصار كبلل بقي في فمه بعد المضمضة لدخوله من الأنف إذا أطبق الفم وفيما ذكرنا إشارة إلى أنه من أدخل بصنعه دخانا حلقه بأي صورة كان الإدخال فسد صومه سواء كان دخان عنبرا أو عودا أو غيرهما حتى من تبخر ببخور فآواه إلى نفسه واشتم دخانه ذاكرا لصومه أفطر لإمكان التحرز عن إدخال المفطر جوفه ودماغه وهذا مما يغفل عنه كثير من الناس فلينبه له ولا يتوهم أنه كشم الورود ومائه والمسك لوضوح الفرق بين هواء تطيب بريح المسك وشبهه وبين جوهر دخان وصل إلى جوفه بفعله...

---

[42] al-Tahtawi, *al-Hashiya `ala Maraqi al-Falah*, 1:444-445.

neglectful, hence people should become [seriously] aware and not consider it similar to smelling rose, its water and musk. There is a clear difference between smelling the fragrance of musk and other perfumes and between something that has a perceptible body of smoke (*jawhar dukhan*) entering one's inside intentionally through one's action..."[43]

Some points:

The discussion in the excerpt translated above refers to smoke that has a shape or form, i.e. *visible* smoke. This is emitted from burning substances such as incenses, aromatic solids, liquid aromatics etc. from whole substances, powdered/granulated or pastes used in ceremonies, religious rites and houses.[44] If this is carried out in the house and one intentionally inhales the smoke, then the fast will be considered violated and a repeat (make up fast [= *qada'*]) will be required but no expiation (*kaffara*). If smoke is accidentally (and hence unintentionally) inhaled such that the smoke travels into the mouth and down the throat, then the fast is not violated.

The discussion also relates to any smoke emitted from substances that are consumed such as tobacco (including smoke from shisha) which again if deliberately consumed violates the fast and will require a repeat (make up fast) but no expiation.

---

[43] al-Shurunbulali, *Maraqi al-Falah*, pp.238-239.
[44] Known in the Indian sub-continent as *agarbatti*.

Finally, if any perfumes, fragrances or scents that have visible smoke are inhaled through the nose, then the fast is violated and a repeat (make up fast) will be required but no expiation.

And Allah knows best.

2. Fasting and Breaking a *Qada'* Fast

Q. what if someone was fasting and broke his fast and then he was making up a fast for the one he had already broken but broke that one as well? What will happen then?

A.

As I understand the question, it is something like this: a person fasts in the month of Ramadan but breaks the fast and while making up for this fast (let us call this *qada'* fast f_1) he then violates f_1. In short, what is the ruling on one who breaks a *qada'* fast?

If this is the scenario, then all that happens is that one must make up again for the fast that one had violated. In this case, no expiation (*kaffara*) will be imposed. As a point, it is not befitting for a Muslim to deliberately break fasts within the blessed month of Ramadan as this is sinful for which sincere repentance (*tawba*) is required.

And Allah knows best.

Q. Making up fasts missed in the past when we were young and weren't on the deen.

A.

If you deliberately missed fasts in Ramadan of past years, then on the condition you were above the age of puberty (= being *baligh*) at that time, then these fasts must be compensated for by a make-up fast which can be paced out and do not have to be made up consecutively.

And Allah knows best.

Q. [1] Voluntary/recommended fasts and combining intentions. [2] Misinformed about *iftar* time and whether that requires *qada'*. [3] Using Ramadan fasts as *qada'* fasts.

A.

A[1]. It is permitted in the School of Imam Abu Hanifa (Allah be pleased with him) to combine the intention of the *qada'* fasts of Ramadan with the 6 days of Shawwal or Mondays and Thursdays. Two intentions will be made: a 'primary' (the major intention to make up a missed fast of Ramadan) and a 'secondary' (the subsidiary intention to perform a *sunna* fast). However, it is better to do each separately.

A[2]. Breaking fast at the incorrect time irrespective of being misinformed or not invalidates the fast. A *qada'* fast will have to be made up but no *kaffara*.

A[3]. One may not use Ramadan as a means of fulfilling expiation fasts (*kaffara*), make up fasts (*qada'*) or intend *nafl* ('voluntary') fasts.

And Allah knows best.

Q. Bro, what's the kaffarah for breaking a fast?

A.

You have not specified the question or clarified it. If you break a fast of the blessed month of Ramadan through say deliberate sexual intercourse, eating and drinking, etc.[45] then you will be liable to pay *kaffara* ('atonement'/'expiation') **and** make up that broken fast. If however, you were fasting a *nafl* ('voluntary') fast or a *qada'* (= 'compensation fast') and you broke it, no *kaffara* is given but that specific fast will have to be made up again. Imam al-Marghinani in *al-Hidaya* states this:

"There is no *kaffara* on fasts other than for those of Ramadan because eating in Ramadan is a more serious a crime than in other times..."[46]	وليس في إفساد صوم غير رمضان كفارة لأن الإفطار في رمضان أبلغ في الجناية فلا يلحق به غيره...

And Allah knows best.

Q. Doing a *Qada'* fast but it was broken. Must one do another new *qada'* of the *qada'* fast?

A.

If a person is keeping a *qada'* (= make up fast) and had to break it for a reason (e.g. one fell seriously ill or a women say began her period) then no extra new fast will be required on top of that *qada'* fast; one just makes up the *qada'* fast that was broken.

And Allah knows best.

---

[45] See al-Shurunbulali, *Nur al-Idah* for some of these invalidators, pp.312-315.
[46] al-Marghinani, *al-Hidaya*, 1:220.

Q. How much do I have to pay for each fast I missed?

A.

I do not quite understand your question. The general rule is that if a person misses a Ramadan fast due to illness, travelling, deliberately missing it, etc. then h/she must make it up later (this = *qada'* fast). If however, a person deliberately breaks h/her fast **after** having begun it, e.g. by eating, drinking, having sex, etc. then an expiation (this = *kaffara*) will be necessary. Imam Ibn `Abidin states:

"[...] as for what necessitates a make-up fast, it is due to the fact of not actually performing the fast and hence the absent of its condition..."[47]

أما لزوم القضاء فلعدم تحقق الصوم لفقد شرطه...

Thus, there is a difference between an *omission* of the fast (not doing it from the beginning) and *contravention* of the fast (breaking one of its conditions having begun the fast). If you have missed performing the fast (i.e. omitted doing it) then you will have to make up a corresponding fast for every one you have missed.

Please clarify the question further.

And Allah knows best.

---

[47] See Ibn `Abidin, *Radd al-Muhtar*, 2:402.

3. Swimming and Fasting

Q. Can I go swimming in Ramadan time? ws

A.

Yes, as long as water does not enter the mouth and down the throat, swimming will be permissible. However, taking caution not to let water enter would be difficult. You could swim after breaking fast.

And Allah knows best.

4. Wet Dream and Fasting

Q. If i slept after eating seheri and then woke up after the fajar time with a wet dream is my fast broken?

A.

No. Emission of semen does not break the fast because it does not resemble sexual intercourse in any way.[48]

And Allah knows best.

---

[48] al-Shurunbulali, *Maraqi al-Falah*, p.310:

(أو أصبح جنبا ولو استمر) على حالته (يوما) أو أياما (بالجنابة)...

"(or of he wakes up in the morning in a state of impurity and even if he continues) in his condition (all day) or a few days..."

5. Mouthwash and Fasting

Q. Can we use mouthwash?

A.

There is no harm in using oral hygiene products such as mouth washes or flosses. With regards more specifically to the type of mouth wash products, if they are alcohol based contents, then it may be better to avoid it but verify it with your local imam of the Mosque.

**Note: that according to the Hanafi school, even if a drop of water falls down the throat due to gargling then the fast is nullified and will have to be made up (*qada'*) but no expiation (*kaffara*) is imposed. Imam al-Shurunbulali writes:

"...or if one accidentally breaks the fast with the water used for gargling in that it seeps down the throat..."[49]

أو أفطر خطأ بسبق ماء المضمضة الى جوفه...

This is the case even if it was unintentional.

And Allah knows best.

---

[49] Ibid., p.245.

6. Thinking of Spouse and Fasting

Q. Thinking about my wife while fasting and being aroused.

A.

Thinking about or looking at your wife while fasting **does not** invalidate it. Even if you thought about her and looked at her and ejaculated in the process (**provided you did not touch your private part [even once] or masturbated**). Imam al-Shurunbulali states in *Maraqi al-Falah*:

"[...] (**Or if he ejaculates by looking**) at the private parts of a woman his fast is not invalidated (**or if he thought about it and even if he continued to look at it and think about it**) such that he ejaculates. This is because [s: thinking and looking] do not resemble sex in any way or form which is ejaculating through direct contact..."[50]

(أو أنزل بنظر) إلى فرج امرأة لم يفسد (أو فكر وإن أدام النظر والفكر) حتى أنزل لأنه لم يوجد منه صورة الجماع ولا معناه وهو الإنزال عن مباشرة...

Fasting is invalidated if: "[...] (**or**) he ejaculates (**through** *takhfidh* or *tabtin*)* or to use his hand (**or**) ejaculating from (**kissing and touching**). There is no *kaffara* based on what we have already mentioned..."[51]

(أو) أنزل (بتفخيذ أو بتبطين) أو عبث بالكف (أو) أنزل من (قبلة أو لمس) لا كفارة عليه لم ذكرنا

---

[50] Ibid., p.658.
[51] Ibid., p.676.

* *takhfidh* is where the wife stimulates her husband with her thighs and *tabtin* is where the wife stimulates her husband with her stomach.

And Allah knows best.

7. Fasting and Backbiting

Q. Does backbiting break the Fasting? I heard some people say it don't.

A.

Yes, it is true that according to the Hanafi School, backbiting does not invalidate the fast but this does not mean that it is permitted to do it.[52] In fact, backbiting (al-ghiba in Arabic) is one of the major sins in Islam and much has been written about this by our scholars.

The Hanafi scholars interpret the wording "invalidate" (yafturna) of the hadith below[53] as referring to loss of reward (dhihab al-ajar)[54]:

"Five things **invalidate** one's fast and break the wudu': [1] backbiting, [2] tale-telling, [3] lying, [4] kissing and [5] the false oath..."[55]	خمس يفطرن الصائم وينقضن الوضوء : الغيبة، والنميمة والكذب والنظر بالشهوة واليمين الكاذبة . ورأيت رسول الله صلى الله عليه وسلم يعدها كما يعد...

---

[52] al-Shurunbulali, *Nur al-Idah*, p.309.

[53] This *hadith* is not authentic anyway but rejected. See Imam al-Nawawi, *al-Majmu` Sharh al-Muhadhdhab*, 6:356.

[54] al-Shurunbulali, *Maraqi al-Falah*, p.239.

[55] Ibn Abi Hatim, *al-`Ilal*, 2:62. a *hadith* with another wording mentions:

"The Messenger of Allah passed by a man cupping another man and both were backbiting someone. He (saw) said: the fast of the cupper and the one cupped have been invalidated (aftara)..." → See al-Bayhaqi, *Shu`ab al-Iman*, 5:2299. The *Hadith* is weak due to an unidentifiable (*majhul*) transmitter.	مر رسول الله صلى الله عليه وسلم برجل يحجم رجلا وهما يغتابان رجلا فقال صلى الله عليه وسلم أفطر الحاجم والمحجوم...

Backbiting must be avoided at all times and it is unhealthy for one's spiritual development that they fall into doing it. Imam al-Ghazali (d.505/1111) mentions in his small treatise (a convenient toolkit for correct fasting) entitled *Asrar al-Sawm* ('The Mysteries of Fasting' - § *Fasting of the Tongue*):[56]

Guarding one's tongue from idle chatter, lying, gossiping, obscenity, rudeness, arguing and controversy; making it observe silence and occupying it with remembrance of Allah (Great and Glorious is He) and with recitation of Qur'an. This is the fasting of the tongue (*fa hadhihi sawm al-lisan*). Said Sufyan: "Backbiting annuls the Fast" (*al-ghiba tafsudu al-sawm*) and Layth quotes Mujahid as saying: "Two habits annul Fasting: backbiting and telling lies" (*khaslatani yafsudani al-siyam al-ghiba wa'l-kadhb*).
The Prophet (on him be peace) said: **"Fasting is a shield; so when one of you is Fasting he should not use foul or foolish talk. If someone attacks him or insults him, let him say: 'I am Fasting, I am Fasting'."**[57]

According to a Tradition: Two women were Fasting during the time of Allah's Messenger (on him be peace). They were so fatigued towards the end of the day, from hunger and thirst that they were on the verge of collapsing. They therefore sent a message to Allah's Messenger (on him be peace) requesting permission to break their Fast. In response, the Prophet, on him be peace, sent them a bowl and said: "Tell them to vomit into it what they have eaten." One of them vomited and half filled the bowl with fresh blood and tender meat, while the other brought up the same so that they filled it between them. The onlookers were astonished. Then the Prophet (on him be peace) said: "These two women have been Fasting from what Allah made lawful to them, and have broken their Fast on what Allah (Exalted is He) made unlawful to them. They sat together and indulged in backbiting, and here is the flesh of the people they maligned!"[58]

---

[56] al-Ghazali, *Asrar al-Sawm*, p.43.
[57] al-Ghazali, *Asrar al-Sawm*, p.44 and Bukhari, *Sahih* (*hadith* no.1904).
[58] al-Ghazali, *Asrar al-Sawm*, p.44:

And from this we take lesson.

And indeed, Allah knows best.

أن امرأتين صامتا على عهد رسول الله صلى الله عليه وسلم فأجهدهما الجوع والعطش حتى النهار حتى
كادتا أن تتلفا فبعثتا إلى رسول الله صلى الله عليه وسلم يستأذناه في الإفطار فأرسل إليهما قدحا وقال صلى
الله عليه وسلم قل لهما قئا فيه ما أكلتما فقاءت إحداهما نصفه دما عبيطا ولحما غريضا وقاءت الأخرى مثل
ذلك حتى ملأتاه فعجب الناس من ذلك فقال صلى الله عليه وسلم : هاتان صامتا عما أحل الله لهما وأفطرتا
على ما حرم الله تعالى عليهما قعدت إحداهما إلى الأخرى يغتابان الناس , هذا ما أكلتا من لحومهم...

The *isnad* is weak according to Imam al-Hafiz al-'Iraqi because there are
unidentifiable transmitters within the *isnad* (chain of transmission), *al-
Haml al-Asfar fi 'l-Asfar*, 1:315.

8. Breaking the Fast with a Cigarette

Q. Is it allowed to break the fast with cigarettes?

A.

The etiquettes of breaking the fast in emulation of the blessed Prophet (Allah bless him and give him peace) include:

1. To eat moist dates (*ratab*) at the point of breaking the fast, if not then
2. Dry dates (*tamr*),[59] if not then
3. Water (*ma'*).

Anas b. Malik (Allah be pleased with him) said:

"The Messenger of Allah (Allah bless him and give him peace) used to have the *iftar* with moist dates before he prayed. If there were not any, he ate dry dates and if there were none he drank water..."[60]	كان رسول الله صلى الله عليه وسلم يفطر على رطبات قبل أن يصلي فإن لم تكن رطبات فعلى تمرات فإن لم تكن حسا حسوات من ماء...

---

[59] Another narration that establishes using dates to break the fast is:

"Whoever finds dates then let him make *iftar* with it; and if not then with water for it is pure..." See Dawud, *Sunan* (#2355); al-Tirmidhi, *Sunan* (#695); Ibn Majah, *Sunan* (#1699); al-Hakim, *al-Mustadrak*, 1:432 (according to the conditions of Bukhari and Muslim with al-Dhahabi agreeing [in his *Talkhis*]) and al-Bayhaqi in *al-Sunan al-Kubra*, 4:238.	إذا كان أحدكم صائما فليفطر على التمر فإن لم يجد التمر فعلى الماء فإن الماء طهور...

[60] Abu Dawud, *Sunan* (#2356); al-Tirmidhi, *Sunan* (#696); Ahmad, *al-Musnad*, 3/164; al-Hakim, *al-Mustadrak*, 1:432 (according to the

4. To use the right hand.
5. To praise Allah and recite the supplication that fasting was for his sake and with His provision (*rizq*).

It is a real shame that often, we fail to adhere to the etiquettes of fasting as outlined in the rush of appeasing our habits. The need to break the fast with a cigarette ought to be a habit that is eliminated (or better still, quitting smoking entirely) and is indicative of our more deeper failures to live by the beautiful standards of our religion.

We ask Allah to enable us to break all bad habits in this month and to observe the requirements of our sacred Law. *Amin*!

And Allah knows best.

---

conditions of Muslim); al-Mundhiri, *al-Targhib wa'l-Tarhib*, 1:151; al-Baghawi, *Sharh al-Sunna*, 3:474 and al-Daraqutni, *al-Sunan*, 2:401.

9. Breaking the Fast Deliberately

Q. what does one have to do if they break their fasting on purpose? And what is their sin for doing that?

A.

There are different areas of fasting that carry different rulings (*ahkam*). Thus, there are acts that:

1. Do not nullify the fast and hence require no *qada'* (make up fast) and no *kaffara* (atonement for the fast).

2. Do nullify the fast that require *qada'* but no *kaffara* and

3. Do nullify the fast that require *qada'* **and** require a *kaffara*.

Both the latter two categories are serious offenses during the blessed month of Ramadan and one must exercise restraint from them. Two of the most common offenses are sexual gratification and eating/drinking. Imam al-Shurunbulali, a famous Judge of the Hanafi School of law (*madhhab*), writes:

"...21 things nullify the fast if a person who is fasting does them willingly and intentionally without being compelled which necessitates the make up fast and the atonement for it. These include: [1.] sexual intercourse in either of the passageways for both the doer and the

باب: ما يفسد الصوم و تجب به الكفارة مع القضاء : و هو إثنان و عشرون شيئا إذا فعل الصائم شيئا منها طائعا متعمدا غير مضطر لزمه القضاء والكفارة و هي : الجماع في أحد السبيلين على الفاعل و المفعول به و الأكل والشرب سواء فيه يتغذى به أو يتداوي...

receiver [2.] as well as eating or drinking regardless of whether it is for nourishment or for a medical benefit...”[61]

Some points:

- [في أحد السبيلين] means in any of the passageways, e.g. the anus or the vagina. > this is regardless of whether one climaxes or ejaculates. The fact of penetration and the completion of the act nullifies the fast.[62]

- [الفاعل و المفعول به] means the doer and the receiver. Thus, both the man and the woman nullify their fast. > this act does not fall under the category of *zina* ('fornication' or 'adultery') as such as it is not unlawful sexual intercourse between unmarried couples or between one spouse's infidelity to another.[63]

- [سواء فيه يتغذى به أو يتداوي] means regardless of whether it is for nourishment or for a medical benefit. Any form of consumption therefore invalidates the fast.

- To carry out any of these actions is a sin against Allah and hence the requirement of atoning for the sin, i.e. 'paying' for the consequences.

- [الكفارة] = *kaffara*: Regarding the atonement/expiation, Imam al-Shurunbulali writes:

"The expiation involves the والكفارة تحرير رقبة ولو كانت غير freeing of a slave even if it

---

[61] al-Shurunbulali, *Maraqi al-Falah*, p.241.
[62] Ibid., p.241.
[63] Ibid., p.241.

is a non-Muslim. And if one is unable to do that, he must fast two consecutive months that do not coincide with the either the two ʿIds or the days of Tashriq. Failing this, then the expiation is to feed 60 unfortunate people who are to be treated to lunch and dinner [at their respective times] so that they are content or [the unfortunate persons] are fed two lunches and two dinners or fed a dinner and a pre-dawn meal. It is also permitted to offer each unfortunate person half a *saʿ* of wheat, flour or one *saʿ* of dates or barely or the value equal to [the above items]. One expiation suffices for sexual intercourse committed on different days as well as eating on different days throughout Ramadan even though these are days of Ramadan of two different years. If however, an expiation has occurred between two acts, then one offer of expiation is not sufficient and this is the most evident view on the matter."[64]

مؤمنة فإن عجز عنه صام شهرين متتابعين ليس فيهما يوم عيد ولا أيام التشريق فإن لم يستطع الصوم أطعم ستين مسكينا يغديهم ويعشيهم غداء وعشاء مشبعين أو غداءين أو عشاءين أو عشاء وسحورا أو يعطي كل فقير نصف صاع من بر أو دقيقه أو سويقه أو صاع تمر أو شعير أو قيمته تداخل الكفارات. وكفت كفارة واحدة عن جماع وأكل متعدد في أيام لم يتخلله تكفير ولو من رمضانين على الصحيح فإن تخلل التكفير لا تكفي كفارة واحدة في ظاهر الرواية.

---

[64] See al-Shurunbulali, *Maraqi al-Falah*, pp.243-244. **Note**: Only the text of *Nur al-Idah* is given in translation.

- The matter of *kaffara* is thus very serious with required particulars.[65]

- The sequence goes as follows:

  1. To free any slave (*raqaba*) - Muslim or non-Muslim.

  2. Failing this (perhaps due to lack of access), two consecutive months (*shahrayn mutatabi`ayn*) of fasting that must not encompass the two `Ids or the 11th, 12th and 13th Dhu'l-Hijja (= *ayyam al-tashriq*).[66]

  3. Failing this (perhaps due to illness or old age) to do either of the following:

A.	B.	C.	D.
60 poor/unfortunate individuals (*miskin*) must be properly fed both at lunch and dinner.	60 poor/unfortunate individuals treated to two lunches each.	60 poor/unfortunate individuals treated to two dinners each.	60 poor/unfortunate individuals treated to dinner and a pre-dawn meal (*sahur*).

  5. Failing this, to give 60 persons equivalent to 1 *sa`* (= 1.6kg) of wheat or flour, or 1 *sa`* (= 3.2kg) of dates or barely.

---

[65] Alahazrat, *al-Fatawa al-Ridawiyya*, 10:595-596.
[66] al-Shurunbulali, *Maraqi al-Falah*, p.244.

- The *kaffara* is to fast 60 consecutive days without excuse. > if one is able, one must do it.

- In the Hanafi School, there is no latitude given for the choice of *kaffara* to make – it must be followed in sequence.

And Allah knows best

10. Lipstick and Fasting

Q. Can one put lipstick on and fast?

A.

It is permitted to put lipstick on and it will not invalidate the fast and if the lipstick rubs off on the lips of her spouse (perhaps through kissing, etc.) his fast will not be invalidated either. As a rule, anything that enters the stomach (*batn*) or anything that takes the ruling of the stomach such as the brain (*al-dimagh*) or enters the normal anatomical channels (mouth, ears, anus, etc.) invalidates the fast.[67] So, unless the lipstick entered the stomach of a person, the fast will remain intact.

And Allah knows best.

---

[67] See al-Kasani, *al-Bada'i` al-Sana'i`*, 2:92-93.

11. Chewing and Feeding a Child

Q. some of us have little children. Obviously a little child cannot keep fast. Are we allowed to break the food into little bits and feed it to the child?

A.

Children according to our sacred law are not required to fast until they attain maturity. If a mother or father has to chew food into little morsels to feed the child, then it is permitted. Imam al-Shurunbulali states regarding one of the disliked acts during fast:

"...and chewing something without an excuse..."[68]
و مضغه بلا عذر...

The condition to note is *bi-la 'udhrin* ('without an excuse'). Thus, feeding small children who cannot digest large pieces of food is a valid reason to chew food in the mouth.

And Allah knows best.

---

[68] al-Shurunbulali, *Maraqi al-Falah*, p.248.

12. Cosmetics and Fasting

Q. Someone told me that putting make up on breaks the fast is that correct?

A.

Putting makeup on does not break the fast and neither do any cosmetics.[69] Thus, as a rule, any substance used to enhance the appearance or odor of the human body such as skin-care creams, lotions, powders, perfumes, lipsticks, fingernail and toe nail polish, eye and facial makeup, permanent waves, colored contact lenses, hair colors, hair sprays and gels, deodorants, baby products, bath oils, bubble baths, bath salts, butters and many other types of products do not break the fast.[70] Of course, what purposes they are used for and with what intention are governed by separate rulings related to *tazayyun* ('beautification').[71]

And Allah knows best.

---

[69] *Fatawa Bareilwi*, p.359.
[70] *Fatawa Bareilwi*, p.359.
[71] See Alahazrat, *al-Fatawa al-Ridawiyya*, 4:592 for a discussion.

13. *Suhur* and Fasting

Q. Salam*** this is going to sound complicated a brother woke up after suhoor time and ate Later he found out that the time had actually passed Whats the hukm on this issue does he fast or is his fast valid what does he have to do? Jzk

A.

If the brother did not know the actual time for *suhur* (pre-dawn meal) had passed and he continued eating only to find out after that he had exceeded the required time, then the fast will be invalid and he will have to (i.e. = *wajib*) make it up (*qada'*) but no *kaffara* (atonement) will be imposed. This is the position of the Hanafi school.[72] The reason being that the action was not one that deliberately voids the fast but it was done through lack of knowledge and unintentional.[73] However, the person should continue as normal, i.e. abstain from eating and drinking.

And Allah knows best.

Q. Salam bro. Do we have to eat the suhoor? My parents said that the fast will not be valid if i dont. Jzk

---

[72] See Ibn ʿAbidin's *Radd al-Muhtar*, 2:405:

(أو تسحر أو أفطر يظن اليوم) أي الوقت الذي أكل فيه (ليلا و) الحال أن (الفجر طالع والشمس لم تغرب) (قوله : أو تسحر إلخ) أي يجب عليه القضاء دون الكفارة؛ لأن الجناية قاصرة وهي جناية عدم التثبت لا جناية الإفطار؛ لأنه لم يفسده...

[73] Ibid., 2:405.

A.

It is not obligatory to eat the pre-dawn meal (*sahur*) but strongly emphasised as it is a *sunna* of the beloved Messenger of Allah (abundant peace and blessing be upon him). Perhaps this is what your parents mean. It is not advised to miss the pre-dawn meal unless there is a really strong need or reason. However, if one does miss it, h/her fast **will not** be invalidated.[74]

There are numerous *ahadith* of the Prophet (abundant peace and blessing be upon him) about the pre-dawn meal one being that narrated by Bukhari in his *Sahih* (#1823) from Sayyiduna Anas (Allah be pleased with him): **"Eat the pre-dawn meal as it is blessed"**. Imam Badr al-Din al-`Ayni al-Hanafi (d.855/1451) the Qadi Muhtasib and *hadith* expert discusses some of the blessings and wisdom behind the pre-dawn meal:

"[The Prophet's] statement 'eat the pre-dawn meal' which we mentioned is a recommended command according to consensus [...] it being a blessing (*baraka*) has many meanings as mentioned [by the scholars]. **The First**: it is a blessing in that it makes [fasting] easy by aiding the fasting [...] **The Second**: it being a blessing means it negates any difficulty [...] **The third**: it being a blessing means it gives strength to fast or do actions during the day or other such things [...] **The Fourth**: it being a blessing	قوله تسحروا قد ذكرنا أنه أمر ندب بالإجماع قوله في السحور قال شيخنا رحمه الله روينا بفتح السين وضمها وهو بالضم الفعل وبالفتح اسم ما يتسحر به كالوضوء والسعوط والحنوط ونحوها قوله بركة قد ذكروا فيها معان الأول إنه يبارك باليسير منه بحيث يحصل به الإعانة على الصوم ويدل عليه قوله ولو بجرعة ماء ولو بتمرة ونحو ذلك ويكون ذلك بالخاصية كما بورك في الثريد والطعام إذا هدى في الحرارة واجتماع الجماعة على الطعام لقوله اجتمعوا على طعامكم يبارك لكم فيه الثاني يراد بالبركة نفي التبعة فيه وقد ذكر

---

[74] Mufti Amjad Ali Azami, *Fatawa Amjadiyya*, 1:391.

means it is a ease and a form of charity which is an increase to eating during the *iftar* [...] [Imam Qadi] `Iyad said that through this blessing perhaps a person who wakes up for the pre-dawn meal will engage in remembrance of Allah (*dhikr*), or perform extra prayers or seek forgiveness or other such additional actions which if he did not wake up for the pre-dawn meal, would otherwise have missed through sleeping or leaving it..."[75]

صاحب الفردوس من حديث أبي هريرة ثلاثة لا يحاسب عليها العبد أكلة السحور وما أفطر عليه وما أكل مع الإخوان الثالث يراد بالبركة القوة عن الصيام وغيره من أعمال النهار الرابع يراد بالبركة الرخصة والصدقة وهو الزيادة في الأكل على الأكل عند الإفطار كما كان أولا ثم نسخ وأصل البركة في اللغة الزيادة والنماء وقال عياض قد تكون هذه البركة ما يتفق للمتسحر من ذكر أو صلاة أو استغفار وغيره من زيادات الأعمال التي لولا القيام للسحور لكان الإنسان نائما عنها وتاركا لها وتجديد النية للصوم ليخرج من الاختلاف وقال ابن دقيق العيد هذه البركة يجوز أن تعودوا إلى الأمور الأخروية فإن اتامة السنة توجب الأجر وزيادته ويحتمل أن تعود إلى الأمور الدنيوية كقوة البدن على الصوم وتيسيره من غير أضرار بالصائم قال ومما يعلل به استحباب السحور المخالفة لأهل الكتاب لأنه ممتنع عندهم وهذا أحد الوجوه المقتضية بالزيادة في الأجور الأخروية...

Thus, there are possible religious benefits and rewards in waking up for the pre-dawn meal so that additional reward is obtained. The Holy month of Ramadan is all about gaining reward and seeking forgiveness and

---

[75] See Imam al-`Ayni, *`Umdat al-Qari Sharh Sahih al-Bukhari*, 10:301 (#3291).

closeness to Allah for the Hereafter. We should desire this above everything else.

And Allah knows best.

Q. Fasting and waking up to eat.

A.

If you are fasting in Ramadan, then it is highly desirable to wake up for *suhur* ('pre-dawn meal') and acquire the *baraka* ('blessing in it'):

"Regarding his statement (**the pre-dawn meal is highly recommended**). This is due to what the *jama`a* except Abu Dawud narrated from Anas who said: The Messenger of Allah (saw) said: **"observes the pre-dawn meal as it contains blessings"**. It is said that what is meant by 'blessing' is acquiring piety and God-consciousness while fasting the next day as well as additional rewards..."[76]

قوله: (ويستحب السحور) لما رواه الجماعة إلا أبا داود عن أنس قال قال رسول الله صلى الله عليه وسلم {تسحروا فإن في السحور بركة} قيل المراد بالبركة: حصول التقوي على صوم الغد أو زيادة الثواب

If however you are a fasting a *nafl* ('voluntary') fast and you miss the time for the pre-dawn meal, then you have the option of either fasting or not fasting.

And Allah knows best.

---

[76] Ibn `Abidin, *Radd al-Muhtar*, 2:419.

14. TV and Fasting

Q. Watching TV during Ramadan and fasting.

A.

It is not unlawful in origin to watch TV, browse the internet or listen to the Radio. Of course, it depends on the contents. Perhaps time would be better spent in servicing one's reward (*thawab*) account in the Hereafter by engaging in supererogatory acts of worship, e.g. reading the Qur'an, making *dhikr*, helping the Mosque or family prepare *Iftar*, etc.

And Allah knows best.

15. Fasting and School

Q. The days are getting longer to fast. What about those of us who are at school and have to study. Especially when we got coursework to do. Can we do the fast later and make it up? Jazakalla.

A.

It is a duty upon all Muslims – male and female – to observe the fast during the blessed month of Ramadan. It can be the case that the demands of our pressured lives and extra-religious commitments (whether in school, work or elsewhere) overwhelm us and make us feel our priorities are to meet these demands over and above everything else – including our personal duties and obligations as laid down in our sacred Law. This is a challenge we constantly face especially living in predominantly non-Muslim environments. But with regards to the question, one may not skip, leave or deliberately break a fast unless there are clear grounds or permissions granted by the Shariah.

Imam Hasan al-Shurunbulali a judge and reputed legal expert of the Hanafi legal school from Egypt writes:

And the fast of Ramadan is **an obligation** on all persons as well **as making up fasts that were missed so long as one meets four conditions** as they are conditions pertaining to the obligation and the injunction of the lawgiver therein and they are called obligatory conditions. They include: **Being Muslim** because it is a condition for the particular Shari`ah rulings to apply;

(وهو) أي صوم رمضان (فرض) عين (أداء وقضاء على من اجتمع فيه أربعة أشياء) هي شروط لافتراضته والخطاب به وتسمى شروط وجوب أحدها (الإسلام) لأنه شرط للخطاب بفروع الشريعة (و) ثانيها (العقل) إذ لا خطاب بدونه (و) ثالثها (البلوغ) إذ لا تكليف إلا به (و) رابعها (العلم بالوجوب) وهو شرط (لمن أسلم بدار الحرب) وإنما يحصل له العلم الموجب

being sane because there is in effect no legal injunction without it; **maturity** because legal responsibility rests on it and **knowing it is a religious obligation**.

[...]

The conditions that make it obligatory to fulfil [the fast] which means discharging the responsibility in the designated time are: **to be free from ill health** based on His (Most High) saying (...*whoever of you is sick or travelling...*)[77]; **free from menstruation and post-natal bleeding** based on what we discussed earlier [in the book] and to be a **resident** as we already clarified. **The conditions that validate the fulfilment of the fast are three**: the condition of **intention** everyday for its designated time; **to be free from whatever contravenes [the fast]**, i.e. whatever is contrary to it such as menstruation and post-natal bleeding based on what was already discussed **and to be free from all that breaks the fast**..."[78]

بإخبار رجلين عدلين أو رجل وامرأتين مستورين أو واحد عدل وعندهما لا تشترط العدالة والبلوغ والحرية وقوله (أو الكون) شرط لمن نشأ (بدار الإسلام) فإنه لا عذر له بالجهل (ويشترط لوجوب أدائه) الذي هو عبارة عن تفريغ الذمة في وقته (الصحة من مرض) لقوله تعالى فمن كان منكم مريضا الآية (و) الصحة أي الخلو عن (حيض ونفاس) لما قدمناه (ولإقامة) لما تلوناه (ويشترط لصحة أدائه) أي فعله ليكون أعم من الأداء والقضاء (ثلاثة) شرائط (النية) في وقتها في كل يوم (والخلو عما ينافيه) أي ينافي صحة فعله (من حيض ونفاس) لما فاتهما (و) الخلو (عما يفسده) بطروئه عليه...

---

[77] See al-Baqara:184.

[78] al-Shurunbulali, *Maraqi al-Falah* with the text of *Nur al-Idah* in bold, pp.230-231.

One of the conditions that obligate fasting then is **to be free from ill health.** There are other specifics related to the matter at hand (e.g. travelling, the elderly, etc.) but the point really is that unless a person is seriously ill, h/she is not excused from fasting. Studying for coursework, exams or tests are not grounds for leaving the fast in Ramadan. One does not have to study during the day but can adjust accordingly at night or early evening. To leave the fast or break it intentionally because of exams is to give preference to study patterns or convenience over an ordained duty of Allah (swt). This is not permitted.

It is also a fact that throughout the centuries, Muslim students have observed the fast and made commitments to their exams, there was never any either or. Thus, it is both possible and achievable from the reality.

And Allah knows best.

16. Football and Fasting

Q. If we got football training can we make fast up later?

A.

We ought to know that Allah legislates for our worldly and spiritual benefits. There is wisdom in what He legislates as a whole even though that may not be apparent to us. We ought to also know that the blessed month of Ramadan does not have to entail giving up one's hobbies or regular physical activities like sports. It may mean however that the time of the regular activity is changed so as not to inhibit and prevent the fast from being observed.

**Note: in general, the *madhhab* (legal school) of Imam Abu Hanifa (Allah be pleased with him) considers it disliked (*makruh*) if one does something that extremely weakens a person to observe the fast.[79] In fact, anything which is deemed to weaken one from performing or carrying out the strict duties laid down in the sacred Shari`a, is considered disliked. This is one of the reasons why our blessed Prophet (Allah bless him and give him peace) prevented his noble *Sahaba* from continuously fasting (*sawm al-wisal*).[80]

Football training sessions are often intense and complete workouts requiring constant hydration throughout. It would be medically unadvisable to enter such training sessions without proper refreshment and hydration facilities - especially in hot weather.

---

[79] al-Kasani, *al-Bada'i` al-Sana'i*, 2:78-79.
[80] Ibid., 2:78.

However, we must remember that Fasting (*al-sawm*) is one of the 5 pillars of Islam, i.e. its foundation and hence ordained by Allah:

"...Islam is built upon five pillars: Belief in Allah and his Messenger, performing the five daily Prayer, fasting the month of Ramadan, paying the *zakat*, making the pilgrimage to the Sacred House (*hajj al-bayt*)..."[81]

بني الإسلام على خمس: إيمان بالله ورسوله، والصلاة الخمس، وصيام رمضان، وأداء الزكاة، وحج البيت...

The rewards too are incalculable. The conditions that obligate the fast are i) being Muslim, ii) maturity, and iii) purity (in the case of women):

"One of the conditions that obligate the fast is being Muslim for fasting, by consensus, is not an obligation for non-Muslims with regard to the temporal laws in that they are not commanded to make up the fast after they become Muslim..."

فَمِنْهَا الْإِسْلَامُ فَلَا يَجِبُ الصَّوْمُ على الْكَافِرِ في حَقِّ أَحْكَامِ الدُّنْيَا بِلَا خِلَافٍ حتى لَا يُخَاطَبُ بِالْقَضَاءِ بَعْدَ الْإِسْلَام...

[...]

"another condition is maturity for fasting in Ramadan is not a duty on the child even if it is discerning because no duty to make up the fast is required even after they attain maturity based on his saying (Allah

وَمِنْهَا الْبُلُوغُ فَلَا يَجِبُ صَوْمُ رَمَضَانَ على الصَّبِيِّ وَإِنْ كان عَاقِلًا حتى لَا يَلْزَمُهُ الْقَضَاءُ بَعْدَ الْبُلُوغِ لِقَوْلِ النبي رُفِعَ الْقَلَمُ عن ثَلَاثٍ عن الصَّبِيِّ حتى يَحْتَلِمَ وَعَنْ الْمَجْنُونِ حتى يُفِيقَ وَعَنْ النَّائِمِ حتى يَسْتَيْقِظَ...

وَعَلَى هذا الطَّهَارَةِ من الْحَيْضِ وَالنِّفَاسِ أنها شَرْطُ الْوُجُوبِ عِنْدَ أَهْلِ التَّحْقِيقِ من مَشَايِخِنَا إذْ الصَّوْمُ الشَّرْعِيُّ لَا يَتَحَقَّقُ من

---

[81] See al-Bukhari, *Sahih* (#4514).

bless him and give him peace): 'the pen has been lifted off three: the little child until it has a wet dream, the mad until he regains consciousness and the one asleep until he wakes up.'[82]"

الْحَائِضِ وَالنُّفَسَاءِ فَتَعَذَّرَ الْقَوْلُ بِوُجُوبِ الصَّوْمِ عَلَيْهِمَا فِي وَقْتِ الْحَيْضِ وَالنِّفَاسِ...

[...]

Moreover, purity from menstruation and post-natal bleeding is a necessary condition according to the experts from our teachers because the legal fast (al-sawm al-shar`i) cannot be realised due to menstruation and post-natal bleeding thus they have been exempted from the fast when both these occur..."[83]

In addition to the above there are conditions of: iv) travelling and v) being elderly and infirm, vi) being sick, etc. Thus, from the above, unless you qualify for anyone of those conditions, you will have to observe the fast as part of the Divine commandment of Allah. The month of Ramadan cannot be changed nor delayed – it has a specific time with specific conditions. Unless you are not able to change your training schedule to the evening, you may not purposefully miss the fast.

---

[82] Abu Dawud, *Sunan* (#4403),
[83] al-Kasani, *al-Bada'i` al-Sana'i`*, 2:86-89.

We ask Allah `azza wa jalla to make us set our priorities right and to enable proper completion of the Fast. *Amin.*

And Allah knows best.

17. Gargling and Fasting

Q. 1. Does gargling water break the fast?

Q. 2. When gurgling (doing 'kulli') the person accidentally takes in water while knowing his [sic] fasting, is fast broken?

A.

There are some actions which if intentionally performed, nullify the fast and some actions which if unintentionally occur also nullify the fast. If even a drop of water falls down the throat due to gargling then the fast is nullified and will have to be made up (*qada'*) but no expiation (*kaffara*) is imposed. Imam al-Shurunbulali writes:

"...or if one accidentally breaks the fast with the water used for gargling in that it seeps down the throat..."[84]

أو أفطر خطأ بسبق ماء المضمضة الى جوفه...

This is the case even if it was unintentional.

As a side point, according to Imam Abu Yusuf there is nothing wrong with rinsing one's mouth with cold water to refresh the mouth even when it is not for *wudu'* ('ritual ablution') although Imam Abu Hanifa considered it disliked.[85] In the *al-Fatawa al-Hindiyya* it states:

"...and according to Abu Hanifa (Allah's mercy be upon him) it is disliked for

...وَعَنْ أَبِي حَنِيفَةَ رَحِمَهُ اللَّهُ تَعَالَى أَنَّهُ يُكْرَهُ

---

[84] al-Shurunbulali, *Maraqi al-Falah*, p.245.
[85] Ibid., p.248.

the one fasting to gargle water (al-madmada) or to rinse water in the nostrils (al-istinshaq) without it being for wudu'. He also considered it disliked to wash the body with water [while fasting] or to pour water on one's head [while fasting], defecate in the water, dress with wet [or damp] clothes whereas Abu Yusuf did not consider these as disliked actions [during the fast]. This is the most evident view and was also mentioned by al-Sarakhsi in al-Muhit.[86]

لِلصَّائِمِ الْمَضْمَضَةُ وَالِاسْتِنْشَاقُ بِغَيْرِ وُضُوءٍ وَكُرِهَ الِاغْتِسَالُ وَصَبُّ الْمَاءِ على الرَّأْسِ وَالِاسْتِنْقَاعُ في الْمَاءِ وَالتَّلَفُّفُ بِالثَّوْبِ الْمَبْلُولِ وقال أَبُو يُوسُفَ لَا يُكْرَهُ وهو الْأَظْهَرُ كَذَا في مُحِيطِ السَّرَخْسِيِّ...

It is Abu Yusuf's opinion however that is widely held because in this matter it accords closer to a *hadith* reported by Abu Dawud that states some of the companions used to say:

"I saw the Messenger of Allah (saw) pour water on his head while he was fasting out of thirst and heat..."[87]

لقد رأيت النبي صلى الله عليه وسلم بالعرج يصب على رأسه الماء, وهو صائم من العطش أو من الحر...

- Thus, to cool one's self down with water does not nullify the fast (e.g. using an icepack, etc...).

- Rinsing the mouth or nostrils does not nullify the fast.

---

[86] al-Nizam et al, *al-Fatawa al-Hindiyya*, 1:198.
[87] Abu Dawud, *Sunan* (#2635); Malik, *al-Muwatta'*, 1/294 (#22) and Ahmad in his *Musnad*, 3/475, 4/63, 5/376, 28, 308 and 430.

And Allah knows best.

18. Kissing and Fasting

Q. i kissed my hubby wiv da tongue; is my ruza still ok?

A.

It is extremely important to know the Islamic rulings (*ahkam*) before we embark on doing any action. We are required to know whether something is either allowed (*halal*) or not allowed (*haram*) before we do it. May Allah enable us to fulfil this! *Amin.*

As far as the question goes, there is vagueness in it. If by kissing by the tongue you mean a passionate French kiss, then this will invalidate (break) the fast. Why? Because a French kiss inevitably leads to an exchange of saliva and the ruling, according to the school of Imam Abu Hanifa (may Allah be pleased with him) is that swallowing or tasting the saliva invalidates the fast:

"**And** another point is **swallowing the saliva of one's wife or** the saliva **of one's friend** because he would have tasted it **but there is no** requirement of expiation (*kaffara*) if it is the saliva of **anyone else** because it would be detested of him..."[88]

(و) منه (ابتلاع بزاق زوجته أو) بزاق) صديقه) لأنه يتلذذ به (لا) تلزمه الكفارة بزاق (غيرهما) لأنه يعافه...

Some points:

- Exchange of saliva and swallowing of it results in the fast being invalidated.

---

[88] al-Shurunbulali, *Maraqi al-Falah*, p.242.

- This also necessitates the expiation (*kaffara*) if it is one's spouse or friend.
- One should be refraining from engaging in these intimate actions during the fast as Ramadan is a month of *imsak* ('refrain', 'restraint', etc.).
- It is not strictly about legal rulings and their conditions only. > we should be aware of what Ramadan demands of us and use it as a means to really strengthen our *nafs* (ego-soul) and curb our passions.

May Allah allow us to get the best of the blessed month of Ramadan and enable us to draw closer to Him. *Amin.*

And Allah knows best.

Q. Can i kiss my husband during Ramzan?

A.

The *madhhab* (legal school) of Imam al-A`zam Abu Hanifa (may Allah be pleases with him) makes a differentiation between a sinful/disliked act that invalidates the fast with a sinful/disliked act that does not invalidate the fast. According to the great Azharite luminary Imam al-Shurunbulali it is extremely disliked to passionately kiss and intimately caress (fondling, stroking, rubbing, etc.) during fasting if there are fears of it leading to sexual intercourse. He writes:

"**And** it is disliked for [the one fasting] **to kiss and caress each other** or engage in lewd and passionate acts and other	(و) كره له (القبلة والمباشرة) الفاحشة وغيرها (إن لم يأمن فيهما على الإنزال أو الجماع في ظاهر الرواية) لما فيه من

things like it **if one is not sure that these will not cause an orgasm or sexual intercourse according to the most evident view on the matter.** This is because the fast will be exposed to depravity and perverseness through the effects of the actions. It is also extremely disliked to kiss passionately like biting [or sucking] one of the lips...”[89]

تعريض الصوم للفساد بعاقبة الفعل ويكره التقبيل الفاحش بمضغ شفتها كما في الظهيرية...

Surprisingly to some, the Hanafi School does not consider spouses looking passionately at each other – even if ejaculation occurs – as invalidating the fast. Imam al-Shurunbulali explains:

“...**or if he ejaculates due to looking** at the private parts of a woman, it does not break [the fast] **or thinking [about it] even if he stared at it or thought about it for a while** such that he has ejaculated. This is because there is no [actual] instance of sexual intercourse and not even a picture or a form resembling it...”[90]

(أو أنزل بنظر) إلى فرج امرأة لم يفسد (أو فكر وإن أدام النظر والفكر) حتى أنزل لأنه لم يوجد منه صورة الجماع ولا معناه وهو الإنزال عن مباشرة ولا يلزم من الحرمة الإفطار وفعل المرأتين بلا إنزال منهما لا يفسد...

---

[89] Ibid., p.249.
[90] Ibid., p.238.

Some points:

- The passionate kissing (*taqbil fahish*), amorous play and intimate caressing between spouses that does not result in an emission of semen will not break/invalidate the fast but it is not encouraged. > Ramadan is a month in which these actions are supposed to be curbed.
- Any form of intimate contact the spouses feel will lead to sexual intercourse or ejaculation is extremely disliked.
- One spouse looking at another even if resulting in an orgasm will **not** invalidate the fast.

Therefore, in answer to the question, to kiss your husband goodbye (or vice versa) or pecking him on the cheek will **not** invalidate the fast.[91]

And Allah knows best.

---

[91] These would be instances of non-passionate kissing.

19. Fasting and Menstruation

Q. salam ***, for women who missed many of their fast due to Hayd, is it obligatory on them to do it immediately in shawwal or can they delay it after the six fasts of shawwal (ie if they don't delay it after, they may also miss 6 fast of shawwal!), ws

A.

It is not obligatory that women immediately make up their missed fasts in Ramadan due to their *hayd* (menstruation). When the *hayd* duration has been completed then they undergo the *qada'* (make up fasts of those missed in Ramadan) in shawwal or wait later in the year when the days are shorter. Although to perform the *qada'* as swiftly as possible is better.

Shawwal fasts are not obligatory, so if for medical reasons the woman is not able to fast the 6 days fast in shawwal, then there is no sin or blame. Alternatively (and this has less reward) one can make the fasts of shawwal their *qada'* fast as well making two intentions (one for the *qada'* and one for the Shawwal fast). But it is highly emphasised to make them separate fasts.

And Allah knows best.

20. Intention and the Fast

Q. what if i wanted to deliberately break my fast but then didn't then do it?

A.

According to the *madhhab* (legal school) of Imam Abu Hanifa (may Allah be pleased with him) the fast is not invalidated. Imam al-Shurunbulali states that amongst one of the 24 matters that does not invalidate the fast is:

"**...or if he intends to deliberately eat but does not do so** because he did not actually carry out the action..."
[92]

(أو نوى الفطر و لم يفطر) لعدم الفعل...

Thus the deliberate intention to eat does not invalidate the fast as long as one does not actually eat something.

And Allah knows best.

Q. Why is that some bengalsi [*sic*] say that we can hav niyot [*sic*] until 12:00 in the afternoon? Where does it say we can do this?

A.

It is true that our parents – especially within the Bengali community – insist on the fast being valid even if we forget to make the intention the night before. Actually, the opinion is sound according to the *madhhab* of our noble

---

[92] Ibid., p.239.

Imam Abu Hanifah (may Allah be well pleased with him) contrary to what some argue. Imam al-Shurunbulali states:

"**As for the type of fast for which it is not conditional upon a specific intention** for the one fasting **or to make the intention at night [prior to the dawn] is Ramadan and vowing to make a fast on a specific day**... and to make the intention at night or during the day before midday is valid..."[93]

(أما القسم الذي لا يشترط فيه تعيين النية لما يصومه (ولا تبييتها) أي النية فيه (فهو أداء رمضان و) أداء (النذر المعين زمانه) كقوله لله علي صوم يوم الخميس من هذه الجمعة فإذا أطلق النية ليلته أو نهاره إلى ما قبل نصف النهار صح وخرج به من عهدة المنذور...

The view is based on evidences and is discussed in detail by Imam Ibn `Abidin in his *Hashiyah*.[94]

And with Allah lies all success.

Q. on intention.

A.

- Intention is a condition of the fast.[95]
- It is simply: "to know in your heart that you are fasting".[96]
- To utter the intention on the tongue is not a condition.[97]

---

[93] Ibid., p.233.
[94] Ibn `Abidin, *al-Radd al-Muhtar*, 2:273f.
[95] al-Mawsili, *Kitab al-Ikhtiyar*, 1:163.
[96] Ibid, 1:163.
[97] Ibid, 1:163.

- The time period in which to make the intention is from when the sun sets (= Maghrib time) the evening before until mid-day the following day.[98]

---

[98] Ibid, 1:163 and 165.

21. Masturbation and Fasting

Q. Does masturbation nullefy [sic] the fast?

A.

Deliberate masturbation (or assisted masturbation, e.g. through rubbing on the thighs, breasts, etc. of one's spouse) leading to ejaculation **does** nullify the fast and a requirement to make it up (*qada'*) is imposed although there is no *kaffara* ('expiation').[99] Imam Ibn `Abidin in his *Hashiya* ('commentary') known as *Radd al-Muhtar `ala 'l-Durr al-Mukhtar* writes:

"The ruling on masturbating with the hands: His statement **this includes masturbation with the hands** is that it does not invalidate [the fast] if there is no ejaculation of semen. However if ejaculation occurs, then one must make up the fast (*al-qada'*) as will be made clear later on and this is the preferred view on the matter as will be discussed [below]...."[100]

مطلب في حكم الاستمناء بالكف: قوله (وكذا الاستمناء بالكف) كونه لا يفسد لكن هذا إذا لم ينزل أما إذا أنزل فعليه القضاء كما سيصرح به وهو المختار كما يأتي...

ونقل في البحر وكذا الزيلعي وغيره الإجماع على عدم الإفساد مع الإنزال واستشكله في الإمداد بمسألة الاستمناء بالكف...

[...]

Consensus was transmitted in [the book] *al-Bahr* [*al-Ra'iq*] and by al-Zayla`i as well as others regarding the fact that ejaculation does not invalidate the fast. A general discussion

---

[99] Alahazrat, *al-Fatawa al-Ridawiyya*, 10:393.
[100] Ibn `Abidin, *Radd al-Muhtar*, 2:399.

is found [in the book] *al-Imdad* under the legal matter of masturbating with the hand..."[101]

Some points:

- According to some hanafi scholars, masturbation itself is not permitted. For example, al-Zayla`i remarks as quoted by Ibn `Abidin:

"What also indicates what we have said is [Imam] al-Zayla`i who advanced the evidence for its impermissibility [of masturbating] with the hand based on Allah's (Most High) statement (...*those who protect their private parts...*) etc to the end of the verse. 'It is not permitted to be gratified in any other way except through one's partner or slave girl.' End [of quotes]. He gave reasons for the impermissibility of seeking [sexual] gratification, i.e. the fulfilment of one's carnal desires except through both types of people. And this is what is apparent to me [from what he has said] and Allah alone knows best"[102]

ويدل أيضا على ما قلنا في الزيلعي حيث استدل على عدم حله بالكف بقوله تعالى { والذين هم لفروجهم حافظون } الآية. و قال فلم يبح الاستمتاع إلا بهما أي بالزوجة والأمة إنتهى . فأفاد عدم حل الاستمتاع أي قضاء الشهوة بغيرهما هذا ما ظهر لي والله سبحانه أعلم.

---

[101] Ibid., 2:399.
[102] Ibid., 2:399.

- However, the jurists were aware of realities (more so today) where temptations are so ubiquitous and the difficulty of avoiding opportunities to gratify one's agitated lust so strong that under a person's honest and overwhelming fear of committing *zina* (illegal sexual intercourse), masturbation becomes permissible but not made a habit.[103] Again, Imam Ibn `Abidin mentions:

"Masturbation is unlawful meaning with the hand if it is to procure lustful desires. As for if one is overcome by extreme lustful desire and he does not have a wife or a slave-girl and he performed [masturbation] in order to relieve himself then there will be no harm or repercussions as stated by Abu 'l-Layth and would in fact be obligatory if he feared committing *zina*..."[104]

(الاستمناء حرام) أي بالكف إذا كان لاستجلاب الشهوة، أما إذا غلبته الشهوة وليس له زوجة ولا أمة ففعل ذلك لتسكينها فالرجاء أنه لا وبال عليه كما قاله أبو الليث، ويجب لو خاف الزنا...

- The rulings given by the scholars are in no way endorsements for doing such actions. > they are responding to actual (and hypothetical) scenarios that require the legal pronouncement (*hukm*) on the particular legal cases (*masa'il*).
- Committing actions that intentionally break the fast is unlawful (*haram*) and one must make sincere repentance to Allah for doing that.
- One must always be engaged in curbing carnal lusts or base desires as allowing these to overwhelm a

---

[103] Alahazrat, *al-Fatawa al-Ridawiyya*, 10:202.
[104] Ibn `Abidin, *Radd al-Muhtar*, 2:47.

person's resolve can be destructive and harmful for spiritual growth.

- There are more detailed discussions of the rulings that can be found in the books of *fiqh*.

And with Allah alone is success.

22. P.E and Fasting

Q. Are we allowed to do P.E. during Ramadan?

A.

It is permitted to perform P.E. during Ramadan but here caution prevails. In general, the *madhhab* (legal school) of Imam Abu Hanifa (Allah be pleased with him) considers it disliked (*makruh*) if one does something that extremely weakens a person to observe the fast.[105] In fact, anything which is deemed to weaken one from performing or carrying out the strict duties laid down in the sacred Shari`a, is considered disliked. This is one of the reasons why our Prophet (Allah bless him and give him peace) prevented his noble *Sahaba* from continuously fasting (*sawm al-wisal*).[106]

On shorter days of fast, some feel that the P.E. lessons add no difficulty to them and carry on doing the lessons. I guess each person's threshold is different. Again, caution is to prevail.

However, if it is possible that your parents are able to provide your school with a letter requesting you be exempted from the lessons often than not, the schools understand and on grounds of religious observance, allow the exemption.

And Allah knows best.

---

[105] al-Kasani, *al-Bada'i` al-Sana'i`*, 2:78-79.
[106] Ibid., 2:78.

23. Swallowing Saliva and Fasting

Q. Does swallowing saliva break the fast? I see people spit in the bin while they're fasting.

A.

There is no harm in swallowing one's saliva while fasting simply because it is unavoidable.[107] It would not be advisable to constantly spit out of fear of invalidating the fast as this can be unsightly (especially in public) and can even increase thirst as loss of moisture in the mouth causes it to dry up. It is also bringing unnecessary hardship for the fast.

Perhaps those who spit saliva when it gathers in the mouth are acting out of conscientiousness to the ruling (*hukm*) that it is *makruh* (disliked) to deliberately gather saliva in the mouth and then to swallow it.[108]

And Allah knows best.

---

[107] Ibid., 2:90.

[108] al-Shurunbulali writes in *Maraqi al-Falah*, p.680:

"**And** it is disliked [for the one fasting] **to gather the saliva in the mouth** deliberately **and then to swallow it** in order to avoid doubts on the character..."

...(و) كره له (جمع الريق في الفم) قصدا (ثم ابتلاعه) تحاشيا عن الشبهة...

24. Kaffara and Fasting

Q. How many Kaffaras does one have to pay for their breaking the fast?

A.

There is some disagreement amongst the scholars of the Hanafi *madhhab* about how many exact *kaffara*/expiation/atonement are to be made for non-performances of past Ramadan fasts or deliberate/intentional violations of fasts. Imam Ibn `Abidin mentions the following:

"Regarding his statement **and he did not make the first expiation**. As for if he did, then any subsequent expiation is binding according to the most evident position [...] It has been mentioned in *al-Bahr [al-Ra'iq]* from *al-Asrar* and before that in *al-Jawhara* that if a person commits sexual intercourse in two different months of Ramadan, then h/she must make the expiation even if the first expiation is not made according to the most evident position and this is the correct view. I say, there is disagreement amongst the scholars as you see it although the second position is stronger because it is the

قوله (ولم يكفر للأول) أما لو كفر فعليه أخرى في ظاهر الرواية للعلم بأن الزجر لم يحصل بالأولى بحر . قوله (وعليه الاعتماد) نقله في البحر عن الأسرار ونقل قبله عن الجوهرة لو جامع في رمضانين فعليه كفارتان وإن لم يكفر للأولى في ظاهر الرواية وهو الصحيح...

قلت فقد اختلف الترجيح كما ترى ويتقوى الثاني بأنه ظاهر الرواية.

most evident position..."[109]

- Shaykh Zadah in his Hanafi manual states:

If a person repeatedly engages in sexual intercourse during days in one Ramadan, and does not fulfil the expiation (*lam yukaffirhu*), then he must fulfil one expiation for it. If he does fulfil the expiation for the first and thereafter makes sexual intercourse again then he must fulfil another expiation [for that] according to the most evident position of the school. If one engages in sexual intercourse in two different Ramadans, then two expiations are obligated as is mentioned from Muhammad [b. al-Hasan al-Shaybani]. However, according to most of the scholars only one expiation is fulfilled and this is the most correct view..."[110]

ولو جامع مرارا في يوم من رمضان واحد ولم يكفره كانت عليه كفارة واحدة فإذا كفر للأولى ثم جامع مرة أخرى فعليه كفارة أخرى في ظاهر الرواية . ولو جامع في رمضانين لزمت كفارتان كما روي عن محمد وقال أكثر المشايخ كفارة واحدة وهو الصحيح...

Thus, some of the senior scholars of the Hanafi *madhhab* have ruled that if a person deliberately does not fast in one Ramadan (say 2007) or deliberately contravenes a fast in it (i.e. breaks it) and does not fulfil the expiation but then in another Ramadan (say 2008) does the same thing, h/she will only be liable to fulfil **one** expiation and no more.

---

[109] Ibn `Abidin, *Radd al-Muhtar*, 2:413.
[110] See Shaykh Zadah, *Majma` al-Anhur Sharh Multaqa al-Abhur*, 1:353-354.

Therefore, as I understand it and Allah indeed knows best, only one *kaffara* is due on any deliberately broken fasts whether they are of two different Ramadans or not.

And with Allah lies all success.

Q. What is the penalty for breaking the roza with sex?

A.

Intentional commission of the act of sex consensually between two Muslims nullifies the fast and incurs two consequences: [1] *qada'* (= 'compensatory fast') and [2] *kaffara* (= 'an expiatory penalty').

(وهي الجماع في أحد السبيلين) أي سبيل آدمي حي (على الفاعل) وإن لم ينزل (و) على (المفعول به)...

"[...] **(and sex in one of the private parts)** i.e. private parts of a living person **(on the doer)** even if no ejaculation occurs **(and)** on the **(receiver)**..."[111]

A few points about *Kaffara*:

- Fasting for 2 months **consecutively** if one starts on the first of a lunar month.
- Fasting for 60 days **consecutively** if one starts any day after the first of a lunar month.
- The fast must not be interrupted (e.g. by Eid, etc.) otherwise it will be invalidated and must be restarted.

---

[111] al-Shurunbulali, *Maraqi al-Falah*, p.664.

- (Women resume their *kaffara* when their *hayd* [menstruation] stops).

And Allah knows best.

25. Tasting and Fasting

Q. Can i taste food during Ramadan?

A.

I presume you mean by the question can one taste the salt/sour levels of food? If this is the case then the answer is that it is disliked (*makruh*) and hence to avoid it is better as stated in *Maraqi al-Falah*:

"**Seven things are disliked for the one fasting: [1.] tasting things** because they expose the fast to being violated even if it is a voluntary fast according to the school..."[112]	(كره للصائم سبعة أشياء ذوق شيء) لما فيه من تعريض الصوم للفساد ولو نفلا على المذهب...

The thing to be extra careful of is not to swallow the saliva from deliberately tasting the food as this will violate the fast. It perhaps may be better to avoid it unless it is extremely difficult not to.

May Allah accept out fast and enable us to perform it correctly. *Amin*.

And Allah knows best.

---

[112] Ibid., p.248.

[14] Fasting and Medical Scenarios

1. Fasting and Pregnancy

Q. i'm pregnant but i'm also fasting. will an ultrasound scan break my fast?

A.

- An ultrasound scan involves an operator placing a transducer probe on your skin over the part of your body to be examined.
- The probe is a bit like a very thick blunt pen.
- <u>Lubricating jelly is put on your skin so the probe makes good contact with the body.</u>
- The probe is connected by a wire to the ultrasound machine and monitor.
- Pulses of ultrasound are sent from the probe through the skin into the body.
- The ultrasound waves then echo ('bounce back') from the various structures in the body.
- The echoes are detected by the probe and are sent down the wire to the ultrasound machine.
- They are displayed as a picture on the monitor.
- The picture is constantly updated so the scan can show movement as well as structure.
- The operator moves the probe around over the skin surface to get views from different angles.[113]

The important point to note is that a jelly like substance is applied to the area to be examined and **will not** invalidate the fast as gels, creams and liquids applied to the skin do not invalidate the fast because the skin is not considered a passageway or bodily cavity (*al-jawf*) like the

---

[113] Adapted from http://www.patient.co.uk/health/Ultrasound-Scan.htm

mouth, nose, ears, vagina and anus. In the *al-Fatawa al-Hindiyya* and *Radd al-Muhtar* it has:

"Whatever enters through the skin of the body such as oils then the fast is not invalidated as mentioned in *Sharh al-Majma*`. Whoever takes a bath in the water and then finds coolness inside him, then his fast is not invalidated. Such is mentioned in *al-Nahr al-Fa'iq...*"[114]

وما يَدْخُلُ من مَسَامِّ الْبَدَنِ من الدُّهْنِ لَا يُفْطِرُ هَكَذَا في شَرْحِ الْمَجْمَعِ وَمَنْ اغْتَسَلَ في مَاءٍ وَجَدَ بَرْدَهُ في بَاطِنِهِ لَا يُفْطِرُ هَكَذَا في النَّهْرِ الْفَائِقِ...

Thus, because the ultrasound scan involves application of a gel on the skin, no nutrients travel to the stomach or brain and so it is permitted.

And Allah knows best.

---

2. Oils and Fasting

Q. Does putting hair-oil on the hair break the fasting?

A.

Putting any oil in the hair, moustache or beard and combing it does not nullify the fast. It has no effects on it.[115]

And Allah knows best.

---

[115] al-Shurunbulali, *Maraqi al-Falah*, p.249.

3. Fasting and Creams

Q. I have a serious rash on my rear side and was wondering if applying any cream or gels breaks my fast. It gets very agitated if i do not apply them medicine.

A.

Yes it is permitted to apply the cream and gel to the agitated area as long as nothing enters that particular passageway.[116]

And Allah knows best.

---

[116] Mufti Mahmud al-Hasan al-Gangohi, *al-Fatawa al-Mahmudiyya*, 10:142 and Mufti Ludyianvi, *Ahsan al-Fatawa*, 4:.440.

4. Fasting and Blood-tests

Q. My dad is diabetic, and because he's not allowed to take his insulin while he is fasting, he has to check his blood level and sugar level. Can he take a blood test while he is fasting?

A.

Yes. Giving blood does not invalidate the fast and testing for blood does not invalidate the fast either. Nothing is entering the body through the anatomical passages (mouth, stomach, etc…). The Central Asian Hanafi jurist Imam al-Bukhari mentions the following:

"…if dry medicines are applied to a wound of the stomach or heard then the fast is not broken but if the medicine is moist then it is nullified according to Abu Hanifa differing with [Abu Yusuf and al-Shaybani]. Most of the Scholars considered breaching of a cavity and thus entry to the stomach or brain [as the condition]…"[117]

وفي الجائفة والآمة إذا داواهما بدواء يابس لا يفسد صومه وإذا داواهما بدواء رطب يفسد صومه عند أبي حنيفة خلافا لهما وأكثر المشايخ اعتبر الوصول إلى الجوف...

Thus, from this ruing I have heard Hanafi *fuqaha'* permit the injection of insulin while fasting or before breaking the fast as long as it is not through the stomach. It may be better to check with your local Imam.

And Allah knows best.

---

[117] al-Bukhari, *al-Muhit al-Burhani*, 2:348.

5. Donating blood and fasting

Q. Does giving blood break the fast?

A.

As a rule, anything which nourishes the body or provides it with strength invalidates the fast, however little. In the case of blood tests (= *al-fasd*), nothing is entering the body; rather what is taking place is an examination of fluid by obtaining or taking *from* the body. Thus, nothing is entering the body's bloodstream or cavities to contravene the fast.[118]

And Allah knows best.

---

[118] al-Shurunbulali, *Maraqi al-Falah*, pp.248-249.

6. Patches and Fasting

Q. Do nicotine patches break the fast? Isn't that like smoking?

A.

As far as i know, nicotine patches do not contravene the fast. Nicotine patches are transdermal adhesives (i.e. patches that are placed on the skin to deliver a specific dose of medication through the skin and into the bloodstream) and are not substances that have their delivery route through the mouth, anus, etc. In the Hanafi School, any substance absorbed through the skin does not invalidate the fast because there is no direct channel of transmission to the brain or stomach from the skin (*al-masam*) and patches, injections and such things are considered to be like oils – their contents enter through the skin. al-Imam al-Mawsili al-Hanafi writes:

"If one eats, drinks or has sexual intercourse forgetfully, or sleeps and has a wet dream, or looks at a women and ejaculates or applies oil and *kuhl* or kisses or backbites or intensely vomits or puts drops on the urethra or dust or a mosquito enters the mouth down the throat or if one becomes in a state of impurity then the fast in all these cases is not broken. As for oil, it is applied to the exterior of the body like water when having a bath..."[119]

وإن أكل أو شرب أو جامع ناسياً، أو نام فاحتلم، أو نظر إلى امرأة فأنزل أو ادهن أو اكتحل، أو قبل، أو اغتاب، أو غلبه القئ، أو أقطر في إحليله، أو دخل حلقه غبار أو ذباب، أو أصبح جنباً لم يفطر...و اما الدهن: فانه يستعمل ظاهر البدن كالاغتسال...

---

[119] al-Mawsili, *al-Ikhtiyar li-Ta`lil al-Mukhtar*, 1:190.

Therefore, nicotine patches do not invalidate the fast.

And Allah knows best.

Q. do nicotine patches invalidate the fast? Is this the same as smoking a cigarette?

A.

With regards to fasting there are at least two points to bear in mind:

1) Anything that enters the body through normal anatomical channels, e.g. nose, mouth, anus, etc. invalidates the fast.[120]

2) Any organ that follows the ruling (*hukm*) of the stomach (*al-batn*) must not be breached, e.g. the brain (*al-dimagh*).[121]

Imam al-Kasani states this condition clearly in his monumental work on Hanafi jurisprudence entitled *al-Bada'i' al-Sana'i'*:

"As for what reaches the body cavity (*al-jawf*) or the brain through normal channels (*makhariq al-asliyya*) like the nose, ears and anus in that one snuffed [something through the nose], entered something through the anus or infused drops in the ear and it reached the stomach or the brain, then	وما وَصَلَ إِلَى الْجَوْفِ أَو إِلَى الدِّمَاغِ مِن الْمَخَارِقِ الْأَصْلِيَّةِ كَالْأَنْفِ وَالْأُذُنِ وَالدُّبُرِ بِأَنْ اسْتَعَطَ أَو احْتَقَنَ أَو أَقْطَرَ فِي أُذُنِهِ فَوَصَلَ إِلَى الْجَوْفِ أَو إِلَى الدِّمَاغِ فَسَدَ صَوْمُهُ...

---

[120] al-Shurunbulali, *Maraqi al-Falah*, p.228.
[121] Ibid., p.228.

one's fast will be invalidated".[122]

Thus, from the above, what I understand the position of the Hanafi School to be on this issue of nicotine patches, morphine patches or nutrient patches (including drips) is the following: If nothing enters into the organs, e.g. stomach, brain etc. through the ears, nose, mouth, anus, etc. then the fast is **not** invalidated. In other words, regardless of whether or not a substance (e.g. liquid nutrients) breached the stomach or brain or reached those organs, the fast will not be invalidated **unless** it entered the body through those delineated anatomical channels.

I am not a scholar and it will be best to consult your local Imam of the mosque or any knowledgeable person (`ailm) for clarification.

And Allah knows best.

---

[122] al-Kasani, *al-Bada'i` al-Sana'i`*, 2:92-93.

7. Fasting and Drips

Q. I need to have a drip attached to me but im not really ill i can still do the fast, is my fast gonna be broken or do i have to fast?

A.

If you mean you are put on an intravenous drip then as far as I know it will not break the fast because the route of transmission of an intravenous drip is the vein where substances (liquids) are fed in.[123] As a rule, any substance transmission through the bodily passages such as the mouth, ears, anus, vagina, etc. invalidate the fast and any substance that reaches the stomach or brain through those bodily channels also invalidates the fast. The skin and veins however are not considered routes like the mouth, ears, anus, nose, vagina, etc and hence any transmission of substances through them will not invalidate the fast.[124] This is based on what was mentioned in the *Fatawa Hindiyya* and *Radd al-Muhtar*:

"Whatever enters through the skin of the body such as oils then the fast is not invalidated as mentioned in *Sharh al-Majma'*. Whoever takes a bath in the water and then finds coolness inside his stomach, then his fast is not invalidated. Such is mentioned in *al-Nahr al-Fa'iq*..."[125]

وما يَدْخُلُ من مَسَامٌ الْبَدَنِ من الدُّهْنِ لَا يُفْطِرُ هَكَذَا في شَرْحِ الْمَجْمَعِ وَمَنْ اغْتَسَلَ في مَاءٍ وَجَدَ بَرْدَهُ في بَاطِنِهِ لَا يُفْطِرُ هَكَذَا في النَّهْرِ الْفَائِقِ...

"It is mentioned in *al-Nahr*: because what is present in his

قال في النهر لأن الموجود في حلقه أثر

---

[123] *Fatawa Bareilwi*, pp.362-363.

[124] *Fatawa Bareilwi*, p.363.

[125] Ibn al-Nizam, *al-Fatawa al-Hindiyya*, 1:203.

throat is an internal effect from the skin which is the breach of the body whereas that which invalidates the fast is only from those passageways based on unanimous agreement..."[126]

داخل من المسام الذي هو خلل البدن

والمفطر إنما هو الداخل من المنافذ

للاتفاق...

And Allah knows best.

---

[126] Ibn `Abidin, *Radd al-Muhtar*, 2:395.

8. Fasting and Illness

Q. My grandmother is extremely ill and bed-ridden. Can she fast and what is the ruling for her?

A.

If your grandmother is extremely ill and unable to fast then are some scenarios to bear in mind because of the lack of clarification in the question:

1. If she attempts to fast in her state of illness and fears for her life or health, she may break her fast and compensate for it later (= *qada'*). There will be no penalty of atonement (= *kaffara*).[127]
2. If she attempts to fast in her state of illness and just cannot do it realising it is too difficult and hard on her, she may break her fast and compensate for it later (= *qada'*). There will be no penalty of atonement (= *kaffara*).[128]
3. If she is physically unable to fast because her health is extremely serious and degenerative, then she may pay the *fidya* (monetary compensation) equivalent of 2.5kg of wheat instead.[129]

Imam Ibn `Abidin writes:

"The author had mentioned 5 things from it: <u>continuing compulsion, fear of destruction or fear of compromising one's intellect whether out of thirst or extreme anger</u> and the severe

وقد ذكر المصنف منها خمسة وبقي الإكراه وخوف هلاك أو نقصان عقل ولو بعطش أو جوع شديد ولسعة حية)

---

[127] al-Mawsili, *Kitab al-Ikhtiyar*, 1:173-174.
[128] Ibid., 1:173-174.
[129] Ibid., 1:173-174.

sting of a snake **(for a traveller)** who is a *shar'i*-traveller even if he is one out of disobedience **(or the pregnant woman or the one suckling)** or a wet nurse according to what is apparent **(she most probably fears for herself or her child)**..."[130]

لمسافر) سفرا شرعيا ولو بمعصية (أو حامل أو مرضع) أما كانت أو ظئرا على ظاهر (خافت بغلبة الظن على نفسها أو ولدها)...

"...on his saying **(he has extreme fear)**: or an escalating illness, or a damaging a limb by it being burned, or a severe pain in the eye, a wound or headache or anything like them or similar to them..."[131]

(قوله خاف الزيادة) أو إبطاء البرء أو فساد عضو بحر أو وجع العين أو جراحة أو صداعا أو غيره ومثله ما إذا كان يمرض المرضى قهستاني ط أي بأن يعولهم ويلزم من صومه ضياعهم وهلاكهم لضعفه عن القيام بهم إذا صام ...

Imam al-Shurunbulali defines the criterion for determining fear (*al-khawf*) if one should feel it:

"Regarding his statement **(if she fears)**: What is meant by 'fear' is the degree of probability ascertained through past experience or a proficient Muslim doctor who is not known to be a *fasiq* (open sinner). Others have said that his probity is a condition as mentioned in *al-*

(قَوْلُهُ خَافَتْ) الْمُرَادُ بِالْخَوْفِ غَلَبَةُ الظَّنِّ بِتَجْرِبَةٍ أَوْ بِإِخْبَارِ طَبِيبٍ حَاذِقٍ مُسْلِمٍ غَيْرِ ظَاهِرِ الْفِسْقِ , وَقِيلَ عَدَالَتُهُ شَرْطٌ كَذَا فِي الْبَحْرِ وَجَزَمَ بِهِ فِي الْبُرْهَانِ فَقَالَ : وَطَرِيقُ مَعْرِفَتِهِ الِاجْتِهَادُ فَإِذَا غَلَبَ عَلَى ظَنِّهِ أَفْطَرَ

[130] Ibn 'Abidin, *Radd al-Muhtar*, 3:461.
[131] Ibid., 3:463.

Bahr. And it is affirmed in *al-Burhan* that: the way to know about [what is or is not considered as 'fear'] is through one's own judgment (*al-ijtihad*). If it is highly likely [that one will be harmed] then he may break his fast. The same holds for when one is informed by a proficient and upright doctor..."[132]

وَكَذَا إِذَا أَخْبَرَهُ طَبِيبٌ حَاذِقٌ عَدْلٌ ا هـ .

And Allah knows best.

Q. Severe illness, Chronic illness and fasting.

A.

If a person is severely/chronically ill such that they are unable to fast, then *fidya* must be given of the amount or the equivalent value of 1.63kg of wheat for each fast. Failing this, one must make the serious intention of paying the total amount of *fidya* when one reaches a financially stable position.

Note: if at any time a person's health is regained or restored such that h/she is able to fast, then the missed fasts paid through *fidya* will have to be made up again.[133]

And Allah knows best.

---

[132] See al-Shurunbulali's *Hashiyat al-Durar `ala 'l-Ghurar* as cited in *Radd al-Muhtar* of Ibn `Abidin, 3:463.
[133] See al-Bukhari, *al-Muhit al-Burhani*, 3:361.

9. Fasting and Seizures

Q. Do epileptic fits break the fast?

A.

Epilepsy is stated as being a **chronic** neurological disorder (meaning unchangeable and fixed) characterised by recurrent and unprovoked seizures. The scope, intensity and nature of these seizures vary and the triggers for an epileptic seizure also vary. In all cases, there is an effect on the brain that may or may not lead to loss of consciousness.

It is clearly stated that if a fasting person loses consciousness (e.g. faints), then the fast is invalidated and will have to be made up later (= *qada'*) and so if the epileptic episode is a complex seizure (involving loss of memory, convulsion, etc. [= 'tonic-clonic seizures']) then the fast is invalidated. The following is stated in the *Maraqi al-Falah*:[134]

(أو أغمي عليه) لأنه نوع مرض (ولو) استوعب (جميع الشهر) بمنزلة النوم بخلاف

المجنون (إلا أنه لا يقضي اليوم الذي حدث فيه الإغماء أو حدث في ليلته) لوجود شرط

الصوم وهو النية حتى لو تيقن عدمها لزمه الأول أيضا (أو جن) جنونا (غير ممتد جميع

الشهر) بأن أفاق في وقت النية نهارا لأنه لا حرج في قضاء ما دون شهر (و) استوعبه

شهرا (لا يلزمه قضاؤه) ولو حكما (بإفاقته ليلا) فقط (أو نهارا بعد فوات وقت النية في

الصحيح) وعليه الفتوى لأن الليل لا يصام فيه ولا فيما بعد الزوال كما في مجموع النوازل

والمجتبى والنهاية وغيرها وهو مختار شمس الأئمة وفي الفتح يلزمه قضاؤه بإقامته فيه

مطلقا...

---

[134] al-Shurunbulali, *Maraqi al-Falah*, pp.247-248.

- If one suffers temporary loss of consciousness (e.g. faints), it is considered as a type of *marad* (medical illness).[135]

- If one suffers a temporary (but sustained) loss of consciousness, e.g. for one whole month, then the ruling is seen as being the same that applies to a person who is in sleep and make up fast will have to be observed.[136]

- The actual day one suffers temporary loss of consciousness (e.g. the day one actually faints) is not made up later.[137]

- If a person suffers from clinical insanity for part of the month, he must make up those days he missed when h/her sanity is regained.[138]

- If a person suffers from clinical insanity for the entire month, h/she does not have to make up all those days missed.[139]

Thus, in light of the above, if the epilepsy is sever and complex and use of medication is necessary and unavoidable during the day and is chronic and permanent (i.e. it is for life, no benefit after attempting to introduce a different regime or medication timetable, etc.), then the person in this kind of situation is incapable of fasting and is exempted from it altogether and h/she can pay the *fidya* of feeding a poor person for every fast that is missed and no *qada'* is made for the number of fast missed.

---

[135] Ibid, p.247.
[136] Ibid, p.247.
[137] Ibid, p.247.
[138] Ibid, p.248.
[139] Ibid, p.248.

And Allah knows best.

10. Eye-drops and Fasting

Q. I have to put cream on my eyes as it gets sore. Does this effect [*sic.*] my fast?

A.

Your fast will not be affected by applying cream on the sore area neither will the fast break if you put eye-drops in your eye.[140] The reason being is that the general rule when it comes to a fast being invalidated is if:

1. One eats.
2. One drinks.
3. One has sexual intercourse.
4. Anything which enters the anatomical passageways (mouth, ears, anus, etc.).
5. Anything which reaches the stomach or the brain.[141]

The general principle related to this ruling is mentioned in the *Durr al-Mukhtar* of Imam al-Haskafi:

"The rule is: whatever enters الضابط وصول ما فيه صلاح بدنه through the bodily cavities لجوفه... and nourishes the body..."[142]

Applying eye-drops or ointment to the eyes does not lead to the stomach and brain and neither does it affect or nourish them. Hence it is permitted to use them.[143] More specifically, in the *Fatawa Alamgiriyya* it states:

"If one drops something of لو أقطر شيئا من الدواء في عينه لا يفطر

---

[140] *Fatawa Bareilwi*, p.371.
[141] *Fatawa Bareilwi*, p.371
[142] al-Haskafi, *Durr al-Mukhtar*, 2:610.
[143] *Fatawa Bareilwi*, p.372.

medicine in his eyes then according to us his fast is not broken..."[144]

صومه عندنا ...

And in the encyclopaedic *al-Bada'i` al-Sana`i'* it has:

"[...] putting eye-colour on the eye docs not nullify the fast even if the taste is found in the throat according to the majority of scholars..."[145]

اكتحل الصائم لم يفسد وإن وجد طعمه

في حلقه عند عامة العلماء...

And Allah knows best.

---

[144] *al-Fatawa al-Hindiyya*, 1:203.
[145] a-Kasani, *al-Bada'i` al-Sana`i'*, 2:93.

10. Cupping and Fasting

Q. Dear ***, does cupping break the fast? = SMS message

A.

No. In the Hanafi school, if both the practitioner of cupping (*hijama*) and the patient are fasting, then there is no harm and the fast will not be invalidated. However, if the cupping is sure to lead to weakening the patient, then it would be advisable to avoid it as it will become disliked (*makruh*). As a rule, anything that weakens the person fasting is considered disliked.[146]

And Allah knows best.

---

[146] See al-Tahtawi's commentary on *Maraqi al-Falah*, p.660:

(واحتجم وهو صائم) رواه البخاري وقال الإمام أحمد يفطاره وتكره الحجامة للصائم إذا كانت تضعفه عن

الصوم أما إذا كان لا يخافه فلا بأس به بحر...

"**(and he performs cupping while fasting)** as narrated by al-Bukhari and Imam Ahmad. Cupping is disliked for a person who is fasting if it weakness him from carrying out the fast but if he does not fear it will, then there is no problem with doing it..."

11. Injections and Fasting

Q. Salam *** are Hanafi permitted to take injection while fasting?

A.

Yes, it is permitted in the school of Imam Abu Hanifa (may Allah be pleased with him) as long as it is not injected directly into the stomach.[147] Usually, injections enter into the bloodstream and not into the organ of the stomach or brain.[148] The same holds for drips which include vitamin or liquid nutrients.

And Allah knows best.

---

[147] See al-Bukhari, *al-Muhit al-Burhani*, 3:348:

وفي الجائفة والآمة إذا داواهما بدواء يابس لا يفسد صومه وإذا داواهما بدواء رطب يفسد صومه عند أبي

حنيفة خلافا لهما وأكثر المشايخ اعتبر الوصول إلى الجوف...

[148] See Abu'l-Wafa' al-Afghani's notes on the *Kitab al-Asl* of Imam al-Shaybani, 2:183:

فهما يعتبران الوصول إلي الباطن من مسلك هو خلقة في البدن لأن المفسد للصوم ما ينعدم به الإمساك

المأمور به. وإنما يؤمر بالامساك لاجل الصوم من مسلك هو خلقة دون الجراحة العارضة وابو حنيفة رح يقول

المفسد للصوم وصول المفطر الي باطنه فالعبرة للواصل لا للمسلك وقد تحقق الوصول هنا وفي ظاهر الرواية

فرق بين الدواء الرطب واليابس واكثر مثايخنا ان العبرة بالوصول...

12. Nose-drops and Fasting

Q. Question: do nose drops and nose sprays break the fast?

A.

Yes. Spraying up the nasal cavity invalidates the fast. The nasal cavity is considered an area from which there can be a route to the brain and throat.[149] For this reason any substance that enters it will render the fast invalid.[150] If however, alternative applications of nasal medication can be arranged such as cream or liquid on a cotton swab applied to the inner lining of the nose, then this would **not** break the fast due to the skin not being considered a passageway breach of which invalidates the fast.[151]

And Allah knows best.

---

[149] *Fatawa Bareilwi*, pp.363-365.

[150] See al-Shurunbulali, *Maraqi al-Falah* with the *Hashiya* of Imam al-Tahtawi, p.672:

(باب ما يفسد الصوم) ويوجب القضاء (من غير كفارة) لقصور معناه العذر وهو سبعة وخمسون شيئا تقريبا

وهي... (أو احتقن أو استعط) الرواية بالفتح فيهما الحقنة صب الدواء في الدبر والسعود صبه في الأنف

والسعوط بضم السين الفعل وبفتحها ما يتسعط به قوله : صبه أي الدواء في الأنف هذا معناه لغة والحكم لا

يخص صب الدواء بل لو استنشق الماء فوصل إلى دماغه أفطر أفاده السيد...

[151] al-Nizam et al, *al-Fatawa al-Hindiyya*, 1:204; Ibn al-Humam, *Fath al-Qadir*, 2:82-83 and *Fatawa Bareilwi*, p.363.

Q. Hay-fever, nasal sprays and Fasting.

A.

Hay-fever sprays are generally used to alleviate cold or allergy symptoms such as nasal congestion (blockage of air passage) where a fine mist is administered into the nasal passage through a pump action device/mechanism.

If you suffer from hay-fever (mild or severe) and use a nasal spray to alleviate the bout of sneezing, then you may have to check with a doctor to find out whether it actually reaches the brain. If it does, then it would not be permitted; if it does not, then it would be permitted.

"Whatever reaches the stomach or the brain from the primary [anatomical] passages like the nose, ears and rear end by pouring drops into the nostrils, being administered an enema or inserting water into his ear and this reaches the stomach or the brain, then his fast is invalidated."[152]

وما وصل إلى الجوف أو إلى الدماغ من المخارق الأصلية كالأنف والأذن والدبر بأن استعط أو احتقن أو أقطر في أذنه فوصل إلى الجوف أو إلى الدماغ فسد صومه

Imam Ibn `Abidin adds the following:

"I say: they did not lay down and stipulate enemas, pouring drops into the nose or inserting water into the ears by it reaching the stomach because of it being clear in it otherwise it ought to be such that if there are remains in the nose and it does not reach the head, his

قلت ولم يقيدوا الاحتقان والاستعاط والإقطار بالوصول إلى الجوف لظهوره فيها وإلا فلا بد منه حتى لو بقي السعوط في الأنف ولم يصل إلى الرأس لا يفطر

---

[152] See al-Kasani, *al-Bada'i` al-Sana'i`*, 2:93.

fast   will   not   be
invalidated..."[153]

And Allah knows best.

[End]

Praise be to Allah,
Abundant blessings on our beloved,
The Messenger of Allah,
His family and Companions
And all who follow them.

Completed in the blessed month of Ramadan with the Help
of Allah, August 2011, London

S. Z. Chowdhury

---

[153] See Ibn ʿAbidin, *Radd al-Muhtar*, 2:402.

KEY REFERENCES

Arabic References:

Ibn `Abidin, *Hashiyat Radd al-Muhtar `ala 'l-Durr al-Mukhtar Sharh Tanwir al-Absar*, 7 vols. Beirut: Dar al-Ihya' al-Turath al-`Arabi, n.d.

——————— *Radd al-Muhtar `ala 'l-Durr al-Mukhtar*, 8 vols. Karachi: H. M. S. Co., 1986.

al-Bahlawi, *Adillat al-Hanafiyya min al-Ahadith al-Nabawiyya `ala 'l-Masa'il al-Fiqhiyya*, Damascus: Dar al-Qalam, 2007.

al-Maydani, *al-Lubab fi Sharh al-Kitab*, 4 vols. Karachi: Kutub Khana, n.d.

al-Haythami, *Majma` al-Zawa'id*, Cairo: Maktbat al-Qudsi, n.d.
——————— al-Haythami, *Majma` al-Zawa'id*, Beirut: Dar al-Kitab al-`Arabi, 1982.

Ibn al-Humam, *Fath al-Qadir li 'l-`Ajiz al-Faqir Sharh al-Hidaya*, 9 vols. Beirut: Dar al-Ihya' al-Turath al-`Arabi, 1997.

al-Kasani, *al-Bada'i` al-Sana'i` fi Tartib al-Shara'i`*, 6 vols. Beirut: Dar al-Ihya' al-Turath al-`Arabi, 2000.

al-Marghinani, *al-Hidaya Sharh Bidyat al-Mubtadi*, 4 vols. Beirut: Dar al-Kutub al-`Ilmiyya, 2000.

Mawlana Nizam, et al. *al-Fatawa al-Hindiyya*, 6 vols. Quetta: Maktaba Majdiyya, 1983.

——————— *al-Fatawa al-Hindiyya*, repr. Beirut: Dar al-Fikr, 1979.

———— *al-Fatawa al-Hindiyya*, 6 vols. Beirut: Dar Ihya' Turath al-`Arabi, 1980.

al-Mawsili, *Kitab al-Ikhtiyar li-Ta`lil al-Mukhtar*, 5 vols. Cairo: Dar al-Ma`rifa, 2000.

al-Nadwi, S. al-*Fiqh al-Muyassar*, Karachi: Zam-Zam Publications, 2009.

Ibn Nujaym, *al-Bahr al-Ra'iq fi Sharh Kanz al-Daqa'iq*, 9 vols. Beirut: Dar al-Kutub al-`Ilmiyya, 1997.

al-Qal`aji, M. et al, *Mu`jam al-Lughat al-Fuqaha'*, Beirut: Dar al-Nafa'is, 2000.

al-Quduri, *al-Mukhtasar* (English-Arabic text, trans. M. Kiani, London: Dar al-Taqwa, 2009).

al-Shurunbulali, *Nur al-Idah* (English-Arabic text, trans. W. Charkawi) n.p. 2004.

———— *Maraqi al-Falah Sharh Nur al-Idah*, Damascus: Maktabat al-`Ilm al-Hadith, 2001.

———— *Maraqi al-Falah Sharh Nur al-Idah*, Beirut: Dar al-Kutub al-`Ilmiyya, 1995.

———— *Imdad al-Fattah Sharh Nur al-Idah*, Damascus, n.p. 2001.

———— *Maraqi al-Sa`adat*, Beirut: Dar al-Kutub al-Lubnani, 1973 and English trans. by F. A. Khan, London: Whitethread Press, 2010.

———— *Sabil al-Falah fi Sharh Nur al-Idah*, Beirut: Dar al-Bayruti, n.d.

Usmani, M. T. *Takmilat Fath al-Mulhim*, 3 vols. Karachi: Maktabat-i Dar al-'Ulum, 1986-1987.

Urdu References:

Khan, Ahmed Reza. *al-'Ataya li-Nabawiyya fi' l-Fatawa al-Ridwiyya*, 6 vols. Mubarakpur: Sunni Darul Isha'at, 1981.

———— *al-'Ataya al-Nabawiyya fi' l-Fatawa al-Ridwiyya*, 12 vols. Faisalabad: Maktaba Nuriyya Ridwiyya.

Ludhianvi, Rashid Ahmad. *Ahsan al-Fatawa*, Karachi: H. M. S. Co, 1398–.

Usmani, 'Aziz al-Rahman. *'Aziz al-Fatawa*, Karachi: Darul Isha'at, n.d.

———— *'Aziz al-Fatawa*, 2 vols. Deoband Fatwa Department, n.d.

Printed in Great Britain
by Amazon